FRANCIS

AND THE

SAN DAMIANO CROSS

MEDITATIONS

ON

SPIRITUAL

TRANSFORMATION

SUSAN SAINT SING, PH.D.

ST. ANTHONY MESSENGER PRESS
Cincinnati, Ohio

Scripture passages have been taken from *New Revised Standard Version Bible,* copyright ©1989 by the Division of Christian Education of the National Council of the Churches of Christ in the U.S.A., and used by permission. All rights reserved. Excerpts from *St. Francis of Assisi: Writings and Early Biographies: English Omnibus of the Sources for the Life of St. Francis,* Marion A. Habig, ed., copyright ©1973, used with permission of Franciscan Press, Quincy, Illinois. All rights reserved.

Cover design by Sandra Digman
Book design by Mark Sullivan

LIBRARY OF CONGRESS CATALOGING-IN-PUBLICATION DATA
Saint Sing, Susan.
  Francis and the San Damiano Cross : meditations on spiritual transformation / Susan Saint Sing.
      p. cm.
  Includes bibliographical references.
  ISBN-13: 978-0-86716-735-1 (pbk. : alk. paper)
  ISBN-10: 0-86716-735-1 (pbk. : alk. paper) 1. Francis, of Assisi, Saint, 1182-1226.
2. Crucifix of San Damiano—Prayer-books and devotions—English. 3. Meditations.
I. Title.

BX4700.F6S263 2006
271'.302—dc22

                                                                    2006012830

ISBN-13 978-0-86716-735-1
ISBN-10 0-86716-735-1

Published by St. Anthony Messenger Press
28 W. Liberty St.
Cincinnati, OH 45202
www.AmericanCatholic.org

Printed in the United States of America.

Printed on acid-free paper.

06 07 08 09 10 5 4 3 2 1

DEDICATION

This book is dedicated to the people of New Orleans and to all of the Hurricane Katrina victims of the Gulf Coast states.

I live on the Florida coast. My family and I suffered through Hurricanes Frances and Jeanne in 2004 and Katrina as a Category One and Wilma as a Category Two in 2005. You bore our suffering as Katrina became a Category Four. And as we watched you dying on the decks of the Superdome and in the flooded streets, my mother, who is eighty-one, said to me, "My three brothers, and your father fought in World War II, and I suffered through the Great Depression in order to make our country great and majestic before the world. And this week, our government's woeful response to this disaster has disgraced America before the eyes of the world. I didn't ever want to live long enough to see this day."

Her words and the catastrophic measure of your suffering are indelibly ingrained in my memory and in my prayers forever. May we never forget that generations of Americans died so that America would be a beacon of hope to the world, not a shadow. I grieve with you. You have been forced to embrace Lady Poverty—may she begin to be kind to you in the mystery of her embrace.

In my own small way, I hope that the words herein will bring some measure of solace and peace.

Susan Saint Sing
Stuart, Florida

CONTENTS

INTRODUCTION

A quiet force. Quiet because its words are no longer audible. Force because when they were heard, the energy within the words changed a man who touched a people that influenced a world. His time was eight hundred years ago. Our time is now. And we listen still—hoping to hear the meaning, if not the sound, of the voice of God. Such is the faith of the humble servant who comes in search of the One greater than oneself. And in that act of approaching—kneeling, hoping, waiting, listening—grace extends its essence through the mist and our souls recognize and respond. Undeniable truth needs no sentence structure—it is. And in that existence is God, who is the way, the truth and the life. Words remain as words until the infusion of the quiet force—the breath of God, the energy of life...

The fundamental problem of the cross is that it *is*, and therefore we must have a response, a reaction to it. Since it *is*, what are we in relation to it? And since it stands for the ultimate sacrifice through violence to peace, the peace of another world, a type of peace we do not know without the cross ("My peace I give you"), then with the statement of the existence of the cross is coupled the fundamental question of the cross, which is, how does it make one a person of peace?

To answer we must look at several things. What is peace? Is it just a state of nonviolence? We tend to think of it as a state of inaction, placidness. We think of it as an inactive space, such as calm water. But what if peace is a force, a quiet force but a powerful one? What if this force is capable of inciting a "riot" of more peace? What if the force of peace is greater than the force of war? Gandhi understood this in our age—and Saint Francis understood this in his age. Francis took a stand of peace in front of wealth by rejecting material possessions, in front of war by seeking to resolve the issues of the war through prayer in the caves of the mountain above Assisi, in front of leprosy by living among the lepers and being spiritually and emotionally healed by those with terminal illnesses, in front of rejection, which he detailed in his parable of perfect joy. These powerful instances of witnessing changed lives, just as surely as swords and bombs. Francis was changed by the cross. His internalization of the San Damiano crucifix altered his being and his understanding.

How then can we use this cross to draw nearer to an understanding of Christ and the relationships we are meant to enter? Francis entered a new path with a new direction, because he gave up his earthly father's vision of riches and glory and because of the relationship he encountered in the embrace of Christ. Christ embraced Francis and Francis returned the embrace. Francis fell in love with—not the crucifixion of Christ—but the love embodied in the crucifixion.

Christ loved the Father and so he did his will. The Father loved his creation, his children, so much that he gave his only son. Mary wept at the foot of the cross. In the symbols on the cross, all the great dramas, aspects and psychological complexities of parental, familial, sibling and romantic love are portrayed. The further dimensions of betrayal, trust, loss, wonderment and glory are symbolically played out on the stage, which is the San Damiano crucifix. There are different sets and players on the stage and we are the audience viewing it; it too has an audience upon it that is both viewing the crucifixion and playing a part in it. Francis walked onto that stage a person who had within him the violence of war, unrest and severe doubts. And on this stage he became a person of peace. His prayer before the crucifix was this: "What will be ours to be and do?"

I intend to provide various avenues and insights, stories and vignettes across multiple perspectives so that you will find, in the experiences expressed here, something that rings true to your own experience, and in that resonance enter into a new, deeper relationship with God and thereby a personal transformation to becoming an instrument of peace.

Francis and Clare's vision together reenters the gates of Assisi with the cross now at Saint Clare's Basilica, to stand as an eternal, internal door for us to enter also. How do we bundle up our lives, such as they are, and walk onto that stage painted among the figures and events of the cross and enter? More, how do we embrace it? And perhaps even greater still, how do we feel it embrace us? Desire, worship, willingness, purity of intent— these are the steps we take as we tread toward the door and stand in vigilance, while we humbly knock until the gate swings open. Once we enter and pass through, we become the door for others, and a passage that welcomes our families, friends and coworkers. The San Damiano cross asks us, as it did Francis, to become part of the mystery of transformation. We come before it as ourselves. We kneel and enter into it. We leave transformed, if only for the moment that we try to grasp the mystery that is greater than ourselves.

Francis felt the warm moistness of breath when he heard Christ on the cross speak: "Go and repair my house, which as you see is falling into ruin." And the cross speaks to us still, beckoning us to repair our lives, our relationships, our failings—in honor of him who gave his life there on the cross so that we could become more in the fullness of his presence—to be instruments of peace. Christ's death and resurrection, celebrated on this gilded cross, is a call to each of us—like Francis—to become great through him. We are called to live and to be like him and ultimately to be transformed.

And therein lies the paradox. The humble servant Francis of Assisi, the one who sought to be poor and little, became great through him. In our seeking we too must be ready for whatever words speak to our hearts, for we know not where they will lead us. Francis left Assisi because of the words. He spoke to a pope and to a leper, to an emperor and to a prostitute. The Word became his words, for such is the language of love: oneness, transformation and joy. Wonder must have rained down upon Francis when he knelt on the stones of San Damiano to hear Jesus on the crucifix speak to him. Let us in turn cast our lives upon the stones to listen, to whisper to the Lover who meets us there, and sing...

CHAPTER ONE

THE CHURCH OF SAN DAMIANO IN FIVE PARTS

...[W]hile he was walking near the church of San Damiano, an inner voice bade him go in and pray. He obeyed, and kneeling before an image of the crucified Savior, he began to pray most devoutly. A tender, compassionate voice then spoke to him: "Francis, do you not see that my house is falling into ruin? Go, and repair it for me." Trembling and amazed Francis replied: "Gladly I will do so, O Lord." He had understood that the Lord was speaking of that very church which, on account of its age, was indeed falling into ruin.

These words filled him with the greatest joy and inner light because in spirit he knew that it was indeed Jesus Christ who had spoken to him.[1]

Filled with joy at the vision and words of Christ crucified, Francis took various pieces of cloth of different colors to sell in the city of Foligno, and he sold not only the wares, but also the horse he was riding. He then returned to the church of San Damiano, found the poor priest, and humbly kissing his hands, told him of what he proposed to do.

The priest was astounded at Francis' sudden conversion and at first he did not believe it. Thinking Francis to be joking, he refused the proffered money, and this was due to the fact that not long before he had seen Francis having a good time with his relatives and friends.

Francis insisted more urgently and begged the priest to receive him as a guest for love of God. Finally the priest consented to his staying on, but, for fear of Francis' relatives, he would on no account accept the money; whereupon Francis threw the coins in through the window, so truly had he come to despise all gain.

While Francis was staying in the priest's house, his father went round inquiring for news of his son. When he heard what had happened and where Francis was, calling together his friends and neighbors, he hurried off to find him.[2]

One cannot appropriately write about the San Damiano crucifix without talking about the church of San Damiano. As a believer in holistic philosophy, I think the entire experience of the following five vignettes formed and prepared Francis for his approach to the cross and opened him to its message, as well as prepared him for death. There is also significant symbolism in Saint Clare and the Poor Ladies living at San Damiano for nearly forty years after his death; in the fact that after his experience of the stigmata, Francis returned to these walls. Of all the many places he could have chosen to rest his head, he asked his brothers to carry him to the walls of San Damiano— to the Poor Clares certainly, but also, to the place of his encounter with the breath and voice of God, perhaps to be inspired by the cross one last time.

It was here, during his last illness, that Francis wrote the cosmic poem, "The Canticle of the Creatures." It was here that he drew inspiration from the well within. The significance of the cross is intimately tied to the tiny church and to the boundless world Francis entered into when he crossed through its Romanesque portal and embraced love. In his youth, San Damiano was the font from which he learned and began his spiritual life; and as he aged, it was the font at which he finally entered understanding. And so he lingered, gathering its richness, internalizing its strength and wisdom, expressing his thoughts and prayers in "The Canticle of the Creatures," before being carried to the Porziuncola to meet Sister Death.

THE CHURCH

This was the church that Francis restored in 1205 after Jesus from the crucifix miraculously spoke to him. It was the first cloister for the Poor Clares and where Francis came in his illness to be cared for by Clare and her sisters at the end of his life. Here he wrote "The Canticle of the Creatures." At his death his body was passed through the small window in the apse to be reverenced by Clare and her sisters one final time. Clare died here in 1253. Her body was later moved to her basilica and a new cloister built in her honor within Assisi's walls. Today San Damiano is occupied by the friars and remains much as it was in the time of Francis and Clare.

My first introduction to the San Damiano crucifix was here in this church where a replica of the cross now hangs. The original rests in St. Clare's Basilica for public view. But when I was living in Assisi it was the tiny church of San Damiano where I loved to come in the afternoon when the tourists and the Assisians were taking a siesta. In the darkness of the last pew I could touch the damp stones and murmur, "Brother Rock." Here, cradled by their strength and shelter, Francis became present to me, and I finally understood what Jesus meant when he said, "…the stones would shout out" (Luke 19:40).

It was at his baptism, amidst all the splendor and wealth of San Rufino, that Francis received the Holy Spirit, but it was here in this poor, crumbling, forgotten ruin that he met God.

The church was probably quiet that day, as it is today. Unabashed, Francis slipped down to the rubble and dust. He had been here before; he wondered why he had come again. Moments passed into hours, but still he sat, legs falling asleep beneath him. He had nowhere else to go but here. This was his home, he belonged here for some unknown reason.

Perhaps it was the solitude. With no one watching his comings and goings he could talk aloud or shout his questions and raise his fist in anger at his confusion and lack of direction since returning from the wars. He could also sink down with tears burning his eyes and sob, "Who are you Lord? Why do you draw me in, as if on a baited line? What could you want of me? I am no one. I don't even particularly care for your ceremony and tithes…yet, I love you."

The dam broke and he stood before the crucifix trying to grasp the suspended wood to feel some comfort, some empathy from the painted, linear wounds. His tears revealed the gilded cross beneath its dust, but still it hung lifeless and dumb. He pushed away, ready to leave, angrily thinking that he had cried out futilely again.

"Francis."

He stopped frozen in his steps.

"Francis!" It was louder.

He knew that voice. He had heard it before in his dreams and at Spoleto. He turned and faced the cross, which now had pulse and depth. Life surged around him as the world echoed his name.

"Go and repair my church, which as you see is falling to ruin around you."

He listened for more. It seemed the universe held its breath for a moment, but now the voice was gone. He heard only the wind in the olive trees. The cross hung lifeless again. He fell to his knees, weeping tears of joy and ecstasy. "Yes, my Lord." At last a sign! Direction and purpose! Not immediately recognizing the breadth of the command, Francis set off to find rocks and mortar to rebuild San Damiano's walls.

Whatever he received in that sacred encounter was the precious impetus to holiness that has been given to so few, yet sought by so many. And as I walked back up the dusty road to Assisi, I could see Francis, running and leaping half-crazed, grabbing people's shoulders and twirling them around in a make-believe minuet of love. Love—that is what Francis met in San Damiano. And that is why he was able to skip lightly in glee rather than walk somberly away from such a weighty command.

THE PRIEST

During Francis' conversion he was moved to pack all he owned onto his horse, ride to Foligno and sell it all to give the money to the poor. Walking back, he passed by the old church of San Damiano, which was in desperate need of repair. (In Francis' time, the little church was more a wayside chapel or a healing shrine dedicated to the Roman physician martyrs, Cosmas and Damian, than a parish church under the bishop. It was not unlike the family-owned chapels along the roads and on the hillsides in Greece and Spain, built in homage to God or some saint and for the spiritual protection and edification of its owners.[3])

Because he thought that the voice from the crucifix meant for him to physically restore this little church, Francis went inside, knelt and kissed the hands of Pietro, the old priest who lived there and offered him the money from the sale of the cloth and the horse. The priest tossed the coins out of the window like sand, knowing full well who Francis was and the riotous life he led with his friends. Francis persisted earnestly until the old priest agreed to take Francis in and teach him of God.

The romanticized legends surrounding Francis' staying at San Damiano with the old priest do not usually include the scenarios based on several facts. One was that Francis' family had a country home near San Damiano and that he probably went to the church to seek protection. As an oblate (Benedictine laypeople who had the protection of the religious order of Saint Benedict) Francis fled to San Damiano in order to stave off the problems of his father and the townspeople.

David Flood, O.F.M., in his article "Social Designs and Admonitions," tells us that in 1203, after the wars with neighboring Perugia that threatened Assisi's power, safety and wealth, the city fathers endorsed a charter urging every Assisian to be productive and supportive of each other's wealth and stature in the name of God and the Holy Spirit.[4] This may sound very self-serving, but it was a time of incessant wars, so it was more self-preservation than greed. The families of Italy were powerful subcultures within the society, very much like feudal England. Therefore the idea of pulling together for the greater good of Assisi put the interest of the town, within whose walls these families lived and were protected, above any one individual family. The concept of pulling together to make the town stronger was in a way a cry to make Assisi great, wealthy and safe, and in so doing, making every Assisian and every Assisi family great, wealthy and safe.

It wasn't such a far-fetched plan, but eventually problems revealed themselves. Such as, into whose hands was all this newfound wealth and power going? It was a tricky business since the church, being a spiritual and mighty political structure in those times, was in direct competition with the already powerful families who were in control and seeking more control, not less. So to have Francis Bernardone walking around the streets throwing *away* riches, laying down his knightly sword, proclaiming "blessed are the poor and weak" rather than "blessed are the rich and strong" was quite an issue. And so his first fledgling steps inside the kingdom of the newly born in Christ had to be taken carefully—as the steps across rocks in a rushing stream, lest he slip irretrievably into a merciless world of ridicule, heresy and shame. Those helping him had to be wary also, lest they got swept up in his youthful exuberance. Enter the old priest...

Though precious little is recorded about the old priest who lived at San Damiano and the time Francis spent there hiding from his father, Pietro Bernardone, until his anger cooled off, I'm sure that Francis must have modeled some of his early spiritual life after him, whoever he was. I like to think that they were two kindred spirits, refugees finding sanctuary in God's house—one, the priest, perhaps at the end of his religious duties, and one, Francis, just beginning his. Their nightly stories most likely dwelled on his family—and the prospects of hiding Francis should Pietro come looking for him with a mob, which he surely would and did—and the literal finding of safety and protection within the confines of a religious dwelling and the rules and spiritual covenants of Christ's representative, a priest. Who knows? If this first encounter with seeking refuge and hiding and spiritual sanctuary had gone sour, perhaps there would have been no great story to tell about Francis. Being the head-strong, frightened, internally upset young man that Francis must have been in those early days, it is likely that his experience of the flesh and blood of Christ in the physical reflection of the church through the priest was positive and inspiring—indeed perhaps formative toward taking Francis to the next level of spiritual confidence and confirmation. The old priest—most likely not in the highest circles of the church hierarchy (or he wouldn't be here outside of the city walls in the first place) would have been an attractive coincidence for Francis, who was himself marginalized at this time. The priest then, is quite a major contributor to Francis' development.

When I was at San Damiano sitting in the courtyard, with swallows swooping and diving under the eaves, I wondered how many times Francis sat here and poured his heart out to this sympathetic, wise old man—who undoubtedly had seen it all in his years. I imagined their conversation to be something like this: "Come here, 'Ceco, sit with me and enjoy the peace of this evening."

And Francis answered, staring blankly at the sunset, "I can't enjoy it, Father, I saw my brother in the piazza today. He made fun of me and threatened me about leaving my family. He says my father's anger grows with each day I am gone."

"So why worry and let it ruin this beautiful night?" the priest said, motioning one arm to Assisi and the other to the dry grass and stones around San Damiano. "They are there and we are here."

And so Francis stayed with the old priest. And as he looked at the priest's worn peasant face with its childlike eyes that laughed and danced in the moonlight, he wished they could stay there forever with just the sky, their Lord and the night. But he wondered deep down inside if such precious things could ever be held onto and if one should even try.

THE GARDEN

The courtyard at San Damiano is tiny. Geraniums burst forth from clay pots around the well, and the eaves and overhangs of the outside walkway are dotted with swallows' nests. From here one can see Mount Subasio and down on the plain, Rivotorto and the Porziuncola. From San Damiano, Clare could see where Francis and the brothers were.

All the journeys Clare made were in her heart. She could be in heaven with her Lord as easily as she could be with Francis in Rome. She had only to turn to the kingdom within her. Francis had taught her this on one of his preaching trips into Assisi before she encountered San Damiano. He said that people could travel the world as pilgrims and own nothing yet have a home everywhere they went by entering into the cell within their hearts. Francis carried his cell with him. Clare found her cell apart from Francis, in this secluded churchyard. She didn't need her cell for a home as Francis did—she always had walls and a roof, a refectory and chapel. She needed her cell for love.

Although she may have followed Francis initially because she was infatuated with his dreams and talk of glory, once she and her sisters were alone at San Damiano Francis grew smaller, though never less cherished in her heart. When she was left alone with love, he who is love emerged. And Clare discovered a whole new world of love and presence in Jesus.

She could always turn to him or frolic with him in the poppies or sit quietly with him long into the night. She could talk and ask his opinion, pray for people, be assured of Francis' safety and be comforted during the sadness of separation. Her Lord was always with her; in him a lifetime's worth of travel and excitement was wrapped up in daily meetings of deep contemplative prayer.

The room within her heart grew until all the brothers and the Poor Ladies, Francis and all the townspeople could fit into her once tiny cell, bursting open its grille as a soul content, while listening love poured out its life and hope to the world. And a courtyard content with geraniums and swallows thrived from an inexhaustible well.

THE DORMITORY

Here is where Clare and the Poor Ladies slept. Here is where Clare had the Blessed Sacrament brought to her and she repelled the Saracens who were threatening to attack the monastery; here is where Clare washed the feet of her sisters; here is where Clare lay ill for over twenty years, yet continued to rise from her sickbed to minister to her sisters; here is where the invalid Clare, unable to attend Christmas Mass, saw the whole Mass and participated in it as if she were there (perhaps the reason she is the patron saint of television); and here is where Clare died. All of this activity, all of this love was done through the strength of the San Damiano crucifix which hung in the room below the dormitory radiating its power upward to where Clare and the sisters spent their nights on the floor, with only meager straw mats to sleep upon in imitation of Christ who had nowhere to lay his head, and in imitation of the crucified Savior who lay upon a rough cross in the room below them.

THE PROTECTION OF THE SAN DAMIANO CROSS

Clare resided at San Damiano from 1212 until her death in 1253. The crucifix remained there until a few years after the death of Clare, when it was moved for protection to the new Monastery of St. Clare within the city walls. For seven hundred years it was kept in the privacy of the monastery, until 1957, when during Holy Week, it was placed on public display and has remained so in the public chapel of San Giorgio at the Monastery of St. Clare in Assisi since 1958. But it did not become a popular and common symbol of the Franciscan charism until the 1980s.

NOTES

[1] Marion Habig, ed., *St. Francis of Assisi: Writings and Early Biographies English Omnibus of the Sources for the Life of St. Francis.* "Legend of the Three Companions," Chapter V, 13 (Chicago: Franciscan Herald Press, 1973), pp. 903–904.

[2] *Omnibus,* "Legend of the Three Companions," Chapter VI, 16, p. 906.

[3] Arnaldo Fortini, *Francis of Assisi* (New York: Crossroad, 1981), p. 215. According to the notes sometime in 1103 the small church of San Damiano was given to the prior of San Rufino.

[4] David Flood, "Social Designs and Admonitions" *The Cord,* volume 55, no. 2, March/April 2005, p. 58.

CHAPTER TWO

ON HIS KNEES

THE CROSS

The San Damiano crucifix is painted on walnut wood to which cloth has been glued. It is a large cross, approximately six and a quarter feet wide and almost five inches thick—nearly life-size when compared to the height of Francis who is reckoned to have been around five feet tall—and in its presence one is compelled (as Francis did) to kneel. "[K]neeling before an image of the crucified Savior, he began to pray most devoutly. A tender, and compassionate voice then spoke to him."[1]

FRANCIS' RESPONSE

To be compelled to kneel prostrate before that which you have come to know as God is a very humbling thing. The scintillating presence of that which is love must have made the hair on Francis' arms stand on end with desire. In fact we know from his own words that he had encountered the omnipresent, omnipotent, omniscient God when he said, "Most high, all-powerful, all good Lord!"[2] And though I have no proof—none of us do—it is my hunch that Francis sought the San Damiano crucifix because it accompanied him. It took away his loneliness, comforted him as only something human could have. Being in the presence of the cross would have been proof to Francis that his ideas were not so far-fetched or off the wall. He could see among the figures on the cross that he was not alone. These others had made a similar journey of discovery and had made it through the chaotic fears of life and failure and ridicule. The figures, the corpus, were his new family now. He would live among them—and did.

His heart was good, his soul open. He was silent in his listening. The presence of God must have been enormous in the chapel that day, or moment of the night, when Francis first approached. There is the moment of true grace, with the words spoken from the cross the climax, but the impetus to seek and to come and to sit and to kneel and to listen must have been electric.

If you close your eyes, can you see the two of them? Christ and Francis. What must Francis have experienced or had written on his heart to sway him to such a radical change? He was different from that moment he went to the church. The encounter with the cross was but part of the musical score—the high point or climax perhaps—but only part of the symphony that Umbria, Tuscany, Rome would ultimately perform.

His was a small body too—not unlike the corpus. We know this from the descriptions in Celano and the frescoes on the wall at Mount Subasio. And the interesting part of being able to eavesdrop through the centuries is that we know what Christ said, but we can only surmise Francis' response. Could it have been anything other than, "Lord, I love you?"

If you whisper these words even once, your life cannot be the same. Francis realized that his life was no longer as he had once imagined, nor certainly as his parents had planned. His life was now to be discovered on the whispers of the wind, in the smell of sweet, dry sunflowers in the Umbria sun, in the heat of the grasses on Mount Subasio that swept his legs with each step he grew more certain of. His was to be a journey of glimpses and wonderings. Is that you Lord? There? Do you want this for me? Am I doing your will? He was to trek the slopes of Mount

Subasio and beyond with only Sister Larks and his instincts to guide him. Grace would become him. He would slip in and out of its embrace, naturally, comfortably. The joy of sensing the presence of God in a world of wild beasts, incantations and merciless war would carry him to the sky, for he had encountered the Beloved and all that the Beloved is and was and will be, and he knew that he was forever part of it. He and the Beloved were one because Christ had died for him. And he wanted to be within the corpus with the other figures—the players on the stage of heaven were there before him, mesmerizing him with their availability, so close he could touch them and have his fingertips among them at least until he would join them there in their worship and story.

OUR RESPONSE

Blessed be the Lord God, Blessed be His Holy Name, Blessed be those who kneel in his presence and know that his presence is right there before them. So many acts of unkindness and uncharitable behavior would never be done if we—as did Francis—lived in the present moment of being one with Christ, to the point where we saw Christ right there, right here, every moment of every day, in every situation—such as he saw in the leper. There is no more argument then, nor justification for war, or anger or abuse. Who among us would kill anything if Christ were standing next to us or Christ was the one we were killing? Is this something of what Francis felt in that prison in Perugia? Would people on death row be executed on tables of steel or burned electrically or poisoned if we saw Christ lying there, too? Who among us would put a gas tablet into that chamber? Harsh images, I know—but no harsher than Francis embracing a leper, or watching Crusaders and Saracens hack each other to death.

This cross at San Damiano, like all crosses, is the "canvas" on which the answers are painted. Francis discovered this, and embraced those answers. That is the difference between Francis of Assisi and us. We can sit and imagine it, but most of the time we cannot or do not enter its embrace. He embraced the mystical Christ, who is more human than we are and whose mystical nature is that it can hide its divinity among us. What must it have been like for Francis, and could be for us, to be so moved for the rest of one's life?

Such love.

NOTES
[1] *Omnibus,* "Legend of the Three Companions," Chapter V, 13, p. 903.
[2] *Omnibus,* "Canticle of Brother Sun," p. 130.

CHAPTER THREE

HEAD BOWED, EYES CLOSED,
NO ONE LOOKING AROUND

THE CROSS

The iconographer draws the eyes last. They are the most important and the primary opening into the figure represented, and they present the look of love. The eyes on this cross are open and gaze upon you. However, one legend states that the eyes of Christ were originally closed, but then opened when he spoke to Saint Francis.

FRANCIS' RESPONSE

The revelation that came to Francis when Christ on the crucifix spoke altered the course of history. This corpus, this cross, holds one's gaze through the air. It looks as if it *is* about to speak. Christ's eyes are engaging and seeking, waiting for a receptive soul. Francis Bernardone was such a soul.

Born to Pica and Pietro Bernardone, the rich young Francis was caught up in the medieval feudal battles of Perugia and the Crusades. His knight's heart sought to defend his town, his family, his honor through blood and warfare. Imprisonment in a subterranean dungeon changed him. Some might go through such an ordeal and harden, but Francis was driven into himself and into the depth of self-doubt. Driven to the hills of Mount Subasio that tower over Assisi and to the plains of Umbria he searched for something, a truth, one thing that was true, because up to that point, up to the wars, everything he had learned about security through wealth and power, had disappointed his expectations. He found the truth one day when he came across the abandoned chapel of San Damiano. The words seared into his heart became indelible. It was all true. He had to follow. What he had heard, he loved and longed for the rest of his life. This way of listening and action, of going and repairing, is symbolized in the icon of the cross. The stories within the borders that define the gold edge of the crucifix are tales of angels and saints, mothers and Romans.

Crucifixion is a messy matter. Francis knew when he accepted the words into his heart that, as with all true communions, blood would mingle. Francis' physical suffering on earth is hard to comprehend in this day of modern medicine. So what revelation can our communion with these iconized stories bring? Each heart must answer as Francis did in the end, "I have done what was mine to do; may Christ teach you what you are to do."[1]

OUR RESPONSE

Michael Wilson writes in his book *Heads Bowed, Eyes Closed, No One Looking Around,* "There are these nights when I could swear it is something more than just electric light that comes from inside the empty Laundromat...that skitters across this wet concrete...."[2] His meditations stem from a realm of wonderment and mystery in a modern urban setting that reflects the spiritual presence of something more than the mundane details of that world. This is important, because as moderns we will never be able to go back eight centuries and experience the San Damiano crucifix as Francis did—in a dilapidated church, in stillness, in private. Our worlds are hectic and full of movement. Much like the surrounding environment of the modern San Damiano crucifix that "rests" now in public view with pilgrims, tourists and tour guides milling about. But those who can look at a laundromat and sense the higher nature of light skittering across the wet concrete will certainly be able to cross the distance of the centuries, slide through time to the moment when the crucifix is still indeed more than just a piece of painted wood; when it is like the light coming from inside something as mundane as a laundromat—more to the eyes and the ears and the soul that looks. A head bowed, eyes closed, no one looking around certainly captures the mood of intense prayer and vigil. Was it Francis' pose? We don't know. We do know it is a posture we can assume as we begin the journey.

In that directive we begin our journey into the stories of the San Damiano crucifix. It is a symbolic map given to us from an artist's creative hand, who, inspired by the ultimate Creator, has meanings pressed down and flowing over for us to embrace. And like the blood from Christ's wounds, we don't want to spill even a drop of what is surely grace.

Our job, as was Francis' eight centuries ago, is to look and to listen. In these gestures are grace, humility and littleness. The act of listening is the beginning of an avenue of transformation. When we look we see this gesture at the top of the cross—a choir of angels, heads cocked in attention, are seemingly listening. Above them is the hand of God, representative of the Holy Spirit, below them the risen Christ having already left the cross that we are gazing upon.

NOTES
[1] *Omnibus*, "Celano, Second Life," 214, p. 534.
[2] Michael Wilson, *Heads Bowed, Eyes Closed, No One Looking Around* (Covington, Ky.: What Reindeer Press, 1984). (This is a self-published book of poetry, which has no page numbers.)

CHAPTER FOUR

NIGHT PRAYER

THE CROSS

One of the most noticeable and distinctive aspects of the San Damiano crucifix is that blood is spurting from the nail holes. This reminds us of the radical nature of the dimensionality of the cross. So, too, Jesus is resurrected. We know this because there is no crown of thorns around his head. In the mystery of death and resurrection, the three-dimensional aspects of time—the past (the torment in the Garden), the present (crucifixion on the rock at Golgotha) and the future (the empty tomb and the resurrection)—are all represented in the San Damiano crucifix in a symbolic way. If we meditate on these aspects of dimensionality in Christ, can we overcome our own fears?

FRANCIS' RESPONSE

For Francis, first and foremost, the cross is, after all, a symbol of the crucifixion. Christ—fully human and yet fully divine—sweated blood in the Garden of Gethsemane when he grappled with the mortal aspects of unthinkable pain and suffering, and Francis saw and perhaps identified with this reference to Christ's fear painted on the cross by the artist. Christ pleaded with his father to let this cup pass him by. Jesus knew the horror that was about to befall him. In this conversation with God, Jesus experienced, perhaps for the first time, rejection. His father did not let the cup pass. His prayer was not answered.

How many times had Francis pleaded and bargained with God or begged in the deepest sincerity that he was capable of for a prayer (perhaps a prayer to be rescued from the subterranean cell) to be answered? Yet they too were sometimes not answered.

Francis of Assisi entered this moment of crucifixion through the stigmata. Perhaps we are not so brave as to ask for such a gift, as Francis did. I know for myself that sometimes, when I lay my head down to sleep at night, fear comes rushing in: the fear of being alone, growing old alone, dying alone. I think of Francis in his caves in the dungeon, in the closeness of the stone walls of San Damiano, and I wonder if he was afraid and had his own special prayers. Jesus seemed to be afraid in the Garden. Was Francis?

He threw his clothes on the stones of the street in front of the bishop to show his disdain for the rich who set out to have only their will be done. The helplessness of not being able to matter haunts. Francis identified with the alone, with the weak, and those unable to defend themselves; and when he knelt before the cross, I wonder what he thought about. Did he pray quietly and gently? Was he reverent, or was he angry? Did he cry within the solitude of the cold damp walls of San Damiano? We don't know how long he prayed there before the crucifix spoke—how many times, how many months or years? Surely not every visit was peaceful. It is the nature of being human to question and wonder and suffer in the void of silence. The silent response of those who could help but don't—those who stand by and watch—the injustice right in front of us is, I think, what Francis might have been revolting against.

The Garden of Gethsemane is the ultimate moment of rejection. Jesus asked and pleaded for this cup to pass, but it didn't. And since Christ is omniscient, he knew the cup was not going to pass. The loneliness of this moment of rejection that his family—the Father and the Holy Spirit—the only beings of his own divine nature, had singled him out, as he had singled himself out for our sake is the moment of salvation. Christ experienced our separation, our aloneness and rejection. Francis called this moment *perfect joy.*

OUR RESPONSE

Christ experienced the depths and confounding nature of both mental suffering and physical suffering. We, in our modern age, do not normally confront the physicality of such barbaric public punishment, as Christ did. It is difficult to comprehend what it is like to carry a cross you will soon be nailed to and hung upon. Can anyone of us really imagine this? Can any of us imagine the intricacies of God's love to humble himself for us in such a fashion? Christ's fear was overridden in the Garden by the acceptance of God's will and love. We are asked, so many times in our far more feeble lives than Christ's, to accept such a fate also. Not in being crucified physically, but in our modern rage of maddening traffic, job concerns, family and societal issues, media and global unrest, we are impacted daily with images not unlike what Mary and Joseph of Arimathea witnessed on the mount. Ours is an emotional and psychological imprint that makes us sweat the blood of anxiety and fear through sleepless nights, fear of being alone when aged, fear of litigation, fear of divorce, concerns for the education and safety of our children, lack of faith in an ever-deteriorating political arena.

So far, time has not separated us from that day on the mount that we do not recognize, in the litmus tests of our souls, the profundity of the moment. Mystery and grace are required to help us in our comprehension, but our own human grasp of loss and rejection also meets us in this mystery and redemption by grace and gives us empathy for Christ on the mount. We as humans can feel a tinge of this rejection when our family members cruelly or thoughtlessly ignore us, ignore how we are getting along or not getting along. This rejection is sometimes experienced by the elderly, the marginalized; it is felt by brothers and sisters who shared happy childhoods for years, and then distance and time alienate them from one another as families grow more and more distant geographically and emotionally. For all, the aloneness is a terrible thing to feel.

I saw this panic on an elderly woman's face once. She was in a nursing home window, and when I walked by with my chocolate Labrador, she lurched toward the window and clawed at the glass, wide-eyed, motioning to my dog. She seemed trapped and terrified in some memory of a time when she must have engaged in a relationship—perhaps much like the one I now share with my dog—with some animal that loved her and whom she loved. The woman in the window clawed at the glass excitedly trying to pet my dog through the pane, and she seemed alarmed that she couldn't reach him. The situation was terrifying to me, as well, as I witnessed this poor soul whom I had seen sitting there in that window day after day for three years, now obviously panicked about an emotion she was suffering and the onslaught of rejection she lived daily as she was forgotten there. It tore me apart. But I was helpless. The desk nurse wouldn't let her out or me in to show her the dog close up. All I can imagine is that she was lost in some world, some garden not unlike Christ's where everyone she was related to had abandoned her to the deepest throes of her own mortality. And its terror was evident.

Did Christ actually sweat blood? Maybe—rejection tears at the sinews of your being when you can no longer love—in

presence and time spent together—those whom you want to love
and be with. You leave by separation, disease, injury or death.
Christ encountered these depths in the Garden for our sake,
and that is the glory of this cross. The garden and the mount of
Calvary were behind him. He had done it. He had risen. The joy
is in the faces of all on this cross. They are witnessing the
Resurrection on Easter morning. As Christians, so should we.

As Saint Paul reminds us in his Letter to the Romans,
Christ's suffering here on earth is for our glory thereafter. We
needn't sweat blood because he did for us. It is for us to
embrace his supreme effort and enter in. Sometimes it seems
that the cross speaks only of the hard issues of being a follower
of Christ. I know for myself that I can get so lost at times in the
suffering, the trials, trying to "discern" what God's will is for my
life, that I forget to live my life. The joy of the resurrected Christ
is ours. It is our inheritance as we are told in Romans:

> When we cry, "Abba! Father!" it is that very Spirit bearing wit-
> ness with our spirit that we are children of God, and if chil-
> dren, then heirs, heirs of God and joint heirs with Christ—if,
> in fact, we suffer with him so that we may also be glorified
> with him. (Romans 8:15–17)

And part of being an heir is the joy of the Resurrection as well
as the cross; but we are often so caught up in being righteous
and good, that we can strain all the fun out of existence, and
worse, we can be judgmental to a fault. We are told to judge no
one and that only God can judge. I know that I have felt this
righteous judgment come over me at times, and when I have, I
have tried to temper my critical nature by understanding
Francis' responses to imperfection, the most notable being the
lepers. Francis goes so far as to see the imperfection of a leper

as perfection. It baffles me at times how much I fail at this concept. It is so easy for me to be critical and judgmental because "I know I am right!" And worse, I can wield my intellect like a sword in order to hurt and to be even more critical of others.

If the San Damiano crucifix says anything to us at all, it says that a group of witnesses to Christ's suffering and resurrection need to give to one another the way he gave to us; and we need to give attention to the growing group of singles, elderly, sick and marginalized within our own families first. If we cannot make the family of Christ that we live within feel welcome and loved, then we do nothing by trying to "give" to a faceless "other" out there beyond our own Golgothas.

We as moderns view the whole of Francis' life—beginning, middle and end. When we read about him we already know him as Saint Francis. But, at the time, Francis would not have known the impact of living in the caves instead of his family home, of giving up his father's wealth, of going to Rome to speak to the pope or of receiving the Lady Clare, whose family knights came to get her back. He would not have known—as we do in our safe objectivity—that he would not immediately contract leprosy when he went to work with and talk to the lepers. Both his fear and his courage must have been enormous. Did he ever kneel in front of this cross and cry because he felt alone? Once he left his family and made his family "his father who art in heaven"—then what? Scary stuff. Yet we know that this cross comforted him—his eyes looked upon it. So did Clare's, and now ours. We think it is Christ looking at us that is the right direction, when, perhaps, it is our turning to look at the cross that is the moment of truth. When the silence speaks, and the void, flush with that inseparable love that floods the crevasses of our broken selves, and satiates us, we yearn to become transparent like the essence emanating from the cross to us. We try to *unskin* ourselves to slip through the thin, holy rarefied air. Spirit to spirit we feel the timeless caress of the Other. Ageless in it, we are never old, never alone, and have no need of power. Seamlessly we are enmeshed as our nature—made spirit—enters in. We have no need to linger in flesh. Our feet fly free to him whose feet are nailed above. The journey, no more than a few steps in height, though Everest-like in stature, we summit in him, through him and with him to the top of the world as we know it, only to find that we are prostrate on the floor.

CHAPTER FIVE

WHAT IS IT WE SEE?

THE CROSS

At the top of the San Damiano crucifix is the hand of God the Father. It is within half a semicircle—again the sign of perfection—with two of the fingers outstretched, which according to some scholars indicates the dual man and God nature of Christ, and with the other three fingers closed representing the Father, Son and Holy Spirit. I wonder, as Francis looked upon the cross, knowing the difficulties with his own father—how he viewed this outstretched hand of his Father in heaven.

FRANCIS' RESPONSE

One can look at the individual aspects of the San Damiano crucifix—such as the gesture of the hand of God, the number and details of the angels, or the imbedded image of the Resurrection in the risen Christ—or one can look at the arrangement as a whole, a trilogy. Surely, the unknown artist who arranged them in the original inspiration did so with a directed intent. Nothing is left to chance. All the images—singularly or in groupings—tell a story.

The hand of God, illustrated here, is symbolized in two outstretched fingers—the index and second finger of the right hand. The gesture is a symbolic statement of God's sovereign and supreme, singular position as the ultimate existence, as well as the blessings coming forth from that gesture–blessings flowing down on all that is below it and part of its mystery of creation. The animated angels are full of life; they seem to be a choir of talking, breathing and living creatures welcoming the risen Christ. In this icon they are the embodiment of spirituality, vibrant with the energy of life, of God and of the Son. These heavenly messengers situated beneath the hand of God, fashioned by God's creative intelligence, are abuzz with their task of witnessing to God's glory, and in that witness, are attending to the details of the fruition of his will. They were the heralds on the mountains when Christ was born in a manger, and they attended him in his tomb. Eternally vigilant, their actions are guided by the interior knowledge pressed into the ethereal nature of their beings. This nature is adoration and service. They wait in adoration; they listen and do. Theirs is the waiting without the need for time, theirs is the listening without doubt and theirs is the doing without hesitation or obstruction.

I knew a Benedictine archabbot named Leopold. He was someone I would tease in our fifteen-year relationship, first as college pastor to college student, then as archabbot to young working adult. He was the Benedictine quotient in my life, just as Francis and Clare had their Benedictine mentors. Father Leopold was my confessor and my wisest sounding board. When he became ill, I was granted permission to enter the cloister and visit him several times before he died. I sang and played my guitar for him, and he tried to sing with me the ancient hymn, the *Ultima*:

When our day of life is ending,
Mary with your Son attending,
Lead us home to thee we call,
Virgin, Mother, Queen of all.

One snowy day in the forested hills around the abbey in western Pennsylvania, I broke off a piece of a blue spruce tree, to take in with me for him to smell and to handle in the sterile confines of his deathbed room. He loved it! For a long, long while he sniffed the pungent balsam odor and delighted in the sticky sap, the cold wet vanishing memory of melting snow, and the sharp blue-silver needles on the tawny limb. Life had entered his room and filled his mind and heart for a few moments with lightness and play. I told him I thought the pine branch, which was covered in snow, was the greatest gift I could bring him. He agreed. I told him that each year, at the first snow, I would know it was he shaking a branch playfully overhead, showering me from a celestial perch.

We left it at that, and when I took my last look at him in his room, his face already turned from me and from all in this world, he was sniffing and admiring the branch both in sadness and delight. At an earlier meeting he had asked me, "Where did it all go—my life?" I was stunned. I felt terrified for a moment that an archabbot wouldn't know the worth of his whole life; and if he didn't know at the end of his life, what possible chance would I have someday? But when I left and saw him the last time, I sensed that he had found his answers and knew he would find the rest soon.

A few days later, sitting alone in my kitchen, as large fluffy white flakes drifted past my window in Southwest Ohio—I knew he had just died, just then at that moment. I saw, in my mind's eye four angels, beautiful handsome androgynous creatures, one at his head, one at his feet and two at his sides wrapping him, attending to him, preparing him. Their care and the solemn respect of their task sank into the sinews of my heart. When I called the archabbey, they told me that Leopold had died just a few minutes before.

I sat a long while that morning listening to the sounds of my house in winter. I watched the snow pile up on the window-panes and followed the tracings of a cardinal over the snow-laden branches of the mulberry tree outside. To be a listening aspect of the day is to receive the magnitude of silence in the thunderous impact and elegance of a snowflake. Leopold had entered into the silence of the needles and snow. The four angels met him there, and I continue to listen for his wisdom in the whispers of the winter wind.

Surely, the artist of this crucifix sat in silent wonder, if at no other moment, then when he had completed the masterpiece. It does snow on occasion in Assisi, and I am certain that angels attend to the hopes and dreams and prayers of all the pilgrims that travel there and kneel in front of this same image, as Francis did eight centuries ago.

Perhaps Francis sat or knelt before it in the hushed silence of snowfall. Did this insular experience heighten his prayer, his wonderment? Did he feel angels near him? Was this the Father and brother he could embrace? The timeless nature of this cross speaks to us still if we wait in silent wonder. Its message is a message for the ages, for the church. Though spiritually based, the church is of human structure, and there will always be cor-ruption, there will always be times of low morals and times when it seems the message is falling apart and in need of reform and repair. This is the natural tendency and course of events throughout the two thousand years of the church's existence. But God always restores the message, speaks again the message of the cross of San Damiano. Its message, addressed to those who kneel and pray, is "Go and repair my house which, as you see, is falling into ruin." It is intended for us individually, because we are the churches in ruin. Intuitively we know this. Great writers have touched upon it and invited us into their mystical insights to help us see it. Shakespeare calls this tragic part of us "bare ruined choirs" in Sonnet 73.

OUR RESPONSE

I don't think there is much difference between life and death. The difference is as a leaf suspended in a flowing stream. The stream has movement and force, power. The leaf, as it is carried along in the stream, like the palm of your hand, can be palm down or palm up—same leaf, same hand; only, at one moment in time the leaf has one side up and one side down. There is no difference in the up or down. The moment of turning, which we call death or birth, from one to the other is the difference, and it is only a second in time—a moment of dynamic transition—not a static state at all. And we flow in this stream of life that is the energy of God.

So how then can we correctly "see" the Resurrection? Life, death, life? The dual nature of the San Damiano crucifix is before our eyes—in its essence. It is death and life. The cross tells us Christ is dead, but the paintings of images tell us Christ is alive. The transitional moment in the stream has turned the leaf from one side to another as time carries it along, and on Easter Sunday morning the leaf turns once again. The stages are largely irrelevant; the significant aspect is to remain in the stream, to remain in the grace of God. The image of the paint on the cross is but a slender aspect of the cross, like the edge of a leaf. The nature of the cross is twofold: the surface story (like the changing of the leaf's color in the fall) and the structure of its inner, physical nature. This cross is not unlike us. We are of a multidimensional nature. We appear to one another as who we are—our faces, our voices, our temperaments and talents. Our bodies are the physical structure of our nature. Yet we, since we live, are as the leaf in the stream of life, we are animated from a third source, the *ruah*, the breath of God, the energy of God.

Since the cross is all about dying and death and resurrection, it seems appropriate to address these mystical yet real things. When I was once asked what I thought about death, I replied that I didn't think it meant that much to God. My friend asking the question seemed shocked and wanted to know what I meant. I told her that it is my understanding that God is energy (energy that cannot be created or destroyed, only changed in form). Since God is a continuum without beginning or end, then God is an entity that continues forever. And if we are in God and God is in us, then we will never end. We are but the two sides of the leaf—one side for a moment, which is our mortal state, and the other side, death, which is only a momentary state in the continuum where the life energy is returning to its maker to be transformed into life again. The energy that is life is God and the state of death and the state of life are merely the mortal flesh animated by the life energy or not—until the next energy enlivens another state of flesh, as the continuum is forever. The energy we experience as the uniqueness of self is really the multifaceted face of God. We are the momentary mortal aspect of God in our lifetime. And at the moment of our death, God's spirit returns to its purest state—the energy of spirit. This energy with our unique expression that we feel as self is the creativity of the Creator, flowing through our mortal condition and waiting at the portal of our free will to flow freely, harmoniously with all existence—past, present and future.

Our personality is a product of our human nature, infused with the divine, as it was with Christ. We can make choices. We cry. We love. We play. We are athletes, actresses and plumbers, because we are extensions of the limitless possibilities of God expressing God in us.

Why would God seek the infinitesimal? God didn't seek it—God is it. The collective finite particles are the whole. We are the very fabric of God. We are the fabric, which is God. To me this explains the collective unconscious Carl Jung explored—in that we seem to sometimes sense things or have a *déjà vu* moment inexplicably because we *are* part of the continuum of God and all that was and all that will be. Heaven isn't a distant place, it is within us—we carry it in us, the memory of its reality *is* indelibly pressed into the cells of our brain and flesh and it is the knowledge (unconscious knowledge in some, conscious in others) of being in the glory of God—the joy, the rush experienced in the pure essence of God—the center core, if you will, of the continuum of which everything else is only a part. This center is the pure essence of life. It is the moment of life and death and life again, the Power infinite. Where this energy of God is catalyzing all that is, is pure joy. Total oneness with the Maker—love separated by nothing—no flesh, no clothes, no thoughts, no worries or anxieties—just the exhilaration of oneness, acceptance, love. This is the joy of being absolutely happy without need or worry, without pain, without concern of it ever ending or leaving. This is Heaven.

CHAPTER SIX

THE SHAPE OF THE CROSS

THE CROSS

The shape of the San Damiano cross mirrors the floor plan of a Romanesque church, where the altar is located in the center—the heart. At the level of Christ's arms there are many witnesses to the crucifixion. Moving upward, from the rock of the earth at the cross's base, through the peopled earth, the shape narrows above Christ's halo in the region of the heavenly hosts, as if to signify that we humans do not tread there, that it is a place reserved for ethereal beings.

FRANCIS' RESPONSE

The San Damiano crucifix is unique, as was Francis' response to it. In his lifetime Francis was raised as the son of a wealthy cloth merchant, became a knight, was imprisoned, gave up his inheritance, lived with lepers, started the beginnings of the Poor Clares, the Friars Minors and the secular Franciscans, met with a pope, journeyed to Egypt to speak to a sultan, claimed Lady Poverty as his bride, carried the stigmata on his body and was canonized a saint. His is a tough act to follow.

Francis began the long litany of aforementioned events at prayer before this crucifix. The Lord he met, the vision he saw, the courage he was given was enough for him to take the first steps into his journey. One of the greatest attributes of Francis of Assisi is his recognition of that space on the cross that narrows where no humans dare enter because it is intended only for ethereal beings. His reverence for creaturehood is extraordinary. It is as if somewhere in the embrace between Christ and him, Francis saw or knew the hierarchy of the universe and accepted it.

Lowering himself to the plane of the other creatures, he called his body Brother Ass, using the same Brother or Sister salutation for many other things such as Brother Fire, Brothers Wind and Air, Sister Water. His was an inclusive existence because he humbled himself to be counted among the vast multitude of all that was created by the hand of God. For Francis, to have merely been part of God's thoughts enough to be the product of his creative expression was the endpoint, the culmination.

Francis counted himself blessed to be as lowly as a sparrow. We know from his writings and historical record that he identified with being among the creatures, not above them, where most humans place themselves.

OUR RESPONSE

Francis' charge was to go and repair the church; perhaps our charge will be to go and repair our family or our job, our environment or our relationship with someone, perhaps our relationship with God himself. The humility of living as a created being, equal to all others—and not above anyone or anything—gives a unique perspective to everyday existence. Anticipation is also a good thing. It keeps us striving for more—keeps us wide-eyed and seeking. If Francis had not sought again that day, that autumn in the thirteenth century, he would not have been present in the chapel with the cross to hear the command.

Being present, humble, listening, seeking and making the time to sit in silence and wonder at the stillness in the air is part of our call as Christians. We must never lose the childlike zeal of wonder, for in wonder lies joy and humility. One can only be in awe of that which is recognized as being greater. One would not wonder at something mediocre. It is the wondrous that draws us. And to appreciate that which is wondrous we must seat ourselves and see ourselves as below it.

Nothing was left to chance; everything painted on the cross was to have a dual meaning—the surface meaning and the deeper meaning. And in order for the worshiper *below* the cross to ascend to and join with the meaning *on* the cross, one had to be made into the cross' keylike shape. Only in trying to be one with all that is revealed on the keylike surface of the cross would the deeper mysteries held within be unlocked.

Francis' words, "I have done what is mine to do, may the Lord show you what is yours to do," instruct us to search for our own way to stand among the figures of the cross. I think it is important for all of us to expect our own message from the cross. We all bring our own history before it, just as Francis did. His unique way will not be ours. He even tells his brothers at the end of his life to do what is theirs to do because he had done what was his. And when we look upon the cross, we needn't see only the symbols that a Cistercian monk put there in the twelfth century and be limited by the symbols. We can come to this very special cross with an air of expectation that our message will be unique too. As the cross spoke to Francis, so we should expect it to speak to us. The symbols are a visual cue, to be sure, and their meaning a springboard for our imagination and prayer.

The shells around the cross according to scholars are symbolic of heaven—but perhaps they remind you of a vacation you shared at the sea or a gift you were given. These moments are also the grace of God actualized and spun into the fabric and history of our lives, just as the ridges and design and colors of the shells are. The scholar might see the Centurion's servant who was healed or the face of the artist hovering over the shoulder of the figure on the left. You might look at that small face and see a child or yourself, a son, a grandson. I think we should expect wonders in prayer and come before the cross in an attitude of expectation. We are in that union of prayer where we wait and hope to enter or at least to know that the Holy is near. That is enough to know.

I am certain that on the day Francis followed the visual cues of the cross to their endpoint, the tumblers of the universe clicked, the portal opened inside Francis and grace flowed. By making himself available, he was there to hear. Portals open and close around us each day, each moment, and we must grasp them, seize them, for they are the message of our lives. Like a tabernacle, the gold lining is seen only when the door is open. If we remain closed or refuse to yield our will to God, the lining of ourselves remains lackluster. It is the light of God's searing presence that visited Francis in his acceptance of the stigmata on Mount La Verna, a journey that began in San Damiano before the cross. We do not know where our journeys will end either or how many times we will be pierced through; but we can find consolation and joy in knowing that God is near, God is with us, God goes before us. We are never alone, and like Francis, we are called to come.

CHAPTER SEVEN

THE LEPER AND THE SAN DAMIANO CRUCIFIX

THE CROSS

There are many figures on this cross. One of its most unique features is that other humans besides Christ are depicted—Mary the Mother of God and John, under the protection of the right hand of Christ; Mary Magdalene, Mary Clopas, the Centurion under the left hand; Longinus, Stephen, the small face of an unidentified participant—probably the artist—unknown saints, thirty-three figures altogether are on this cross, including the angels. This gathering was painted intentionally by the artist to symbolize the followers Christ had influenced and would influence. So it is with Saint Francis, too. He began a path many others would follow to the foot of this same cross, in the effort of trying to be Christlike. Thousands followed Francis, the Poverello, because he made the Gospel alive to their world and their time. Christ spoke in the Sermon on the Mount, "Blessed are the poor in spirit, for theirs is the kingdom of heaven" (Matthew 5:3), and Francis literally went to live among the poorest of the poor—the lepers.

FRANCIS' RESPONSE

If one reads the words of Saint Francis, the cross of San Damiano actually speaking to him is not mentioned. The early biographers tell us that it spoke to Francis, but Francis himself says that it was through the lepers that Christ's vision for him was revealed. Through the leper the words to "Go and repair my house" were realized. If you think about this, it makes sense and does not detract from the cross of San Damiano at all. What Francis was rebuilding with stones was only the surface of the meaning—the literal. The true church that needed to be rebuilt was the belief of the people in their benevolent loving and merciful God and Father.

The Middle Ages were a time different in many ways from our own. It was a time of many plagues and disease, superstition, no electricity, no modern medicines, no indoor plumbing, no grocery stores. And yet the same contrasts were there. The world of slaughterhouses, plague, suspicion, lepers and cold stood out in strong contrast to the opulence of a bishop's warm hearth or the basilicas of Rome and the glittering power of a knight going to the Crusades. As with us, these stark contrasts undoubtedly stirred Francis' emotions and spirit.

Consider too that the leper might have been someone Francis knew before he or she contracted the disease. The lepers around Assisi were not imported from other lands. They were the townspeople of Assisi and Perugia who were forced to live outside the city walls when all of their families and friends lived inside the walls. This symbolic divide—the wall, the casting out of friends and relatives to the wilds and the forest—must have touched Francis deeply because he was moved to live among them and to internalize the division and isolation they must have felt. In other words, the dichotomy and juxtaposition he saw and felt he embraced and sought to resolve within the emotional and intellectual fabric of his being. Somewhere in that process of sorting out he came to understand what was church, who he was, who was his family, why these people were left outside the walls, why there was war, why he was imprisoned, why he felt these things and others didn't. Somewhere in his caves and in grappling with his inner self, he found peace in the unlikeliest of places: in the voice, the face, the wisdom, the words of a leper.

The early Franciscan sources tell us that it was when Francis met the leper, his real conversion began, and he came to understand God and found peace of soul. What he heard from the cross of San Damiano did not change him until the words "go and repair my house which you see is falling into ruin" became personified in the leper. Perhaps the leper was his neighbor, or one of his teachers, or a relative—we don't know—but we do know that in Francis' words of his experience and encounter, his path was made clear when he met the leper. So, the words of the cross initially led him to the literal meaning of placing one rock on another perhaps, but the deeper meaning which reached his soul came with the encounter with the leper.

And would this not be so? Would twenty-year-olds like Francis' first companion, Bernard of Quintavalle, be so moved that they too would give up their positions and live in rags just because Francis was going to take on the Catholic church and reform it, or that he was going to collect tithes from the poor to give to the coffers of the princes of the church? I doubt that Francis would have been able to sway Bernard or Saint Clare or what was to become countless hundreds of followers by some plan of renewal of the church. No, the message had to be deeper than a social or political move to revise the corrupt structure of church hierarchy. The essence of Francis' credibility was that God was not to be found only in the tithes and pews of churches; the essence of Francis' credibility was that God, Jesus, the Spirit was found in those who the church had neglected or rejected, the ones who couldn't afford the tithes to buy away their sins or buy indulgences to get themselves out of purgatory. Some of these others would have been friends, family members or townspeople they once knew. Would they not be moved to help?

The real church was the Body of Christ alive and well that had left the rigid surface of the hanging cross. The real church was not suspended above the ground. The real church was not to be kept inside walls or protected by men or women inside monasteries. No, the real church was the Body of Christ in the poor and the lepers and the sick and the rejected and marginalized that perhaps had not even heard or seen the inside of a chapel. The church that Francis sought to rebuild was the Body of Christ he saw through and in the eyes of the leper. Christ was there. If the impetus to seek deeper and move to a deeper spiritual level came from the cross at San Damiano, its resolution was found in the caves and grottoes of the lepers.

Francis inspired and moved the well-heeled youths of Assisi to follow him because what he found was credible. His insight burned true to them because it was true to the biblical experiences of Jesus Christ recorded in the New Testament. That is why the pope heard and approved of what Francis and his followers were doing. He knew that the true church was the people of God, including the poor and the lepers—not just those who entered religious life or those who could afford the tithes of the church or those who implemented the burdens of the church, such as the Crusades, the Spanish Inquisition or the punishments of heretics. These did not speak of the love and mercy that Christ spoke of in the Sermon on the Mount: *Blessed are the poor in spirit, blessed are the peacemakers, blessed...*

If ever anyone or any group were poor in spirit, it would have been the lepers. No, Francis felt love from the cross at San Damiano, and that love spoke to him in more than mere words, and the "church" he described to his friends was the church of peace and gentle care and unity with those who were being sin-gled out and separated. Love does not divide, nor does it lay heavy burdens upon, nor does it label. Christ spoke to Francis in a language that Francis could reveal and communicate to oth-ers readily, easily, so easily that thousands heard it—because it was the light "burden" of love and not the heavy burden of judg-ment and division. The harsh words that enflame and lead to wars and killing and imprisonment Francis had just encoun-tered in his own subterranean internment. No, his world, was going to be above the ground. He was going to travel light on this planet, be a light, not a weight or anchor or shackle.

OUR RESPONSE

Love frees. Hatred and stern harsh words and actions do not. We in our modern world see this in the likes of Gandhi and Nelson Mandela, Mother Teresa. In their littleness they have become global heroes because our unconscious recognizes them as Christ, as love, as reflections of the Father. Others, though powerful and wielding swords of fire and brimstone and heralding peace through war and freedom through death are what Francis ran from. He laid down his sword, gave up his knightly clothes and rejected power because it is not of God cru-cified nor is it of God resurrected. Christ healed everyone who came to him, even when they did not ask. He was the mightiest man on earth and he killed no one, passed judgment on no one but hypocrites, and died on a cross with the request to us to give up all we have and to follow him, be like him. Being like Christ means embracing lepers and living without power and position. The trappings of the church did not impress Francis. Instead he sought the pigsties and mud huts of the poor and laborers. His was a world righted by being upside down. His understanding of the crucifixion would blow us away—because it meant being crucified with our own mores and the social values we create and hold so dear and work so hard to get.

No, the words from the cross were not the endpoint; they were merely the beginning, the breath needed to speak the volumes that Francis' life went on to speak. *Blessed are the poor in spirit for theirs is the kingdom of God* is clear as a bell. Francis the knight, the soldier of Christ fighting for freedom, laid down his weapons because he understood that the violence of the cross superseded him. Francis discovered that the violence of the cross, the war that rages on the corpus of Christ in his wounds, in his words, and in his blood spilled, is the war each of us must enter into and win within our own souls and hearts and minds.

The violence of the cross is the giving of all of oneself in a lifetime of nonviolence.

CHAPTER EIGHT

THE RESPONSIBILITY OF KNOWING

THE CROSS

There are two small figures painted near the larger figures in the center of the cross. They are considered to be Longinus and Stephanos. Longinus on the right and Stephanos on the left are both observing and witnessing the revelation unfolding, just as they did when they were on Golgotha. For Longinus, the Roman centurion who according to legend pierced Christ's side, "...one of the soldiers pierced his side with a spear, and at once blood and water came out" (John 19:34). And for Stephanos, who gave Jesus water from his sponge, the prophecy is fulfilled when Jesus said, "I am thirsty" (John 19:28).

FRANCIS' RESPONSE

Entering into the revelation of the cross had to be a turning point in Francis' personal perspective and relationship with his mother, his father, his friends and Assisi. He needed to be different because he *was* different now; he had touched the grace of the presence of God, and because of that proximity to the Holy, he would lead a somewhat lonely and misunderstood life—except by the others who followed him.

No doubt it was very difficult for him to walk down the streets in this myopic little village of Assisi and see friends and family doing what they had always done, even what he had done, just even a few days before when he was riding horses, laughing, playing and having lavish dinners. But now, if for no other reason than being pensive about what he had encountered, Francis most certainly would have been a very different young man. He inexplicably knew in an instant of grace what many would never know in a lifetime of striving to understand: Everything in the Bible was true and was real. And because he carried this indelible knowledge within himself, he had the responsibility of acting upon it, of letting it nudge him into becoming a different person, a gentler person, perhaps; less judgmental, but for certain, he would have felt that he was different and walked on a path that others did not see. He had not done it out of his own will or desire. He had not entered this realm because he was somehow worthy or better than anyone else. In fact, because Francis did carry this knowledge of the closeness and magnitude of God's grace, if anything, he felt even more minuscule, more imperfect and more aware than ever of his sins. He couldn't have possibly felt anything other than this.

OUR RESPONSE

The simple act of having his inner self juxtaposed with the crucified Christ in that moment of exchange of grace would have clarified his role and indeed all of our roles—immediately. We are as nothing compared to God; and Francis knew this, felt this, and at times, I suspect was even bothered by it—because it is an alien perspective to what we normally experience.

Each of us normally experiences our families, friends or ourselves as a cohesive unit. We belong to this unit, biologically and emotionally, yet now, in an instant Francis was intimately part of the kingdom of God, the family of the Holy Spirit and an heir to the kingdom of heaven (certainly, a major change of perspective for anyone to grapple with or to grasp). It must have made him pause many times to feel this distinction and know that he couldn't really explain it or give it away or wish it onto anyone else. It was what it was because it was of God's doing.

One of the aspects of the San Damiano crucifix's speaking to Francis that has always kept me wondering is the weight of responsibility Francis must have felt after hearing the call to "go and repair my house which is falling into ruin." We associate with the physical response that Francis gave of physically rebuilding the wood and stone structure, and we associate with the global quality of "church" meaning repairing the infrastructure of the church by being a new spiritual leader; but I am taken aback at times wondering how Francis, the person, the young man, felt—one on one—with the responsibility of knowing he was singled out. There is a tremendous responsibility to respond, better than the next person, simply because you *do* know there is a God and this God has just spoken to *you*.

Once you are singled out, you must make yourself be better than you were before it, or why would the cross's words mean anything at all? We see the physical rebuilding of structure. We see the global, spiritual call for Francis as a new leader of a new way of living the gospel to inspire the whole world. But it is the singular moments in Francis' mind, when perhaps the wind was just lightly blowing through his hair, and the sun was hot on his forehead as his nostrils filled with dry grass and ginestra, that he felt the weight of knowing that *he*, just one person, was called. He would have to accept that from the day the crucifix spoke; from that day forward, he had a responsibility to weigh the actions of others on a different scale than he had in all his previous life. He sensed, no doubt, what Jesus alluded to when he said, "Prophets are not without honor except in their own country and in their own house" (Matthew 13:57).

CHAPTER NINE

RAREFIED AIR

THE CROSS

In the heavens above Christ's head on the San Damiano cross is an assemblage of ten gesturing angels who seem to be monitoring, observing and perhaps attending the happenings on earth below them. They seem vigilant, poised, content and encouraging.

FRANCIS' RESPONSE

If you read the early writings of Francis and his brothers, often you will come upon passages that allude to the fact that Francis, because of physical pain, torment over sin and anxiety did not sleep that well at night. Did he hope and pray that these angels would watch over him? Did his decision to follow the words of Christ—to rebuild—ever keep him up? Pivotal decisions in one's life usually do. They are hard to make, and Francis, though pursuing saintliness, was very much a human. Gut-wrenching decisions typically feel as if there are hard, irretrievable edges that cannot be gone back over once crossed. The leap of faith is scary. Once Francis started rebuilding San Damiano and gave his clothes back to his father, the die was cast. He would find his direction and peace through the journey of discovering just how solid the ground was under his feet. The confirmation that his leap was indeed of God's will and not his own would come clear only through the journey, and the journey was to be his reward.

Inward journeys are the hardest of all. In the Franciscan classic, *Francis: The Journey and the Dream,* Murray Bodo writes,

> At first, this inner search was a painful and terrifying look at himself, at his weakness and sinfulness; and the journey was a downward dive that made him feel that he was drowning in some vast, bottomless lake. But as he persevered in prayer, he came at last to something like a great, silent, waterproof cavern in which the sound of his own voice seemed mellow and deep; and there at that depth within, Jesus spoke softly to him and made his heart burn with love.[1]

Symbolically, the caves and cavelike structures in Francis' life are like the *kivas* of the Pueblo people, the holy places of transformation for the passage of rights of initiation. He had the experience of confinement and conversion from war in the prison at Perugia. He had the caves of Mount Subasio where he first sought shelter and peace from the demons and thoughts that ripped at his soul after the war. He had the prisonlike cave of the subterranean room his father locked him in at Chiesa Nuova, and the cavernly nature of the little church of San Damiano whose walls were damp and whose stones were insular and close around him. He sought womblike protection, which is an interesting symbol in that he had turned from the warlike or more masculine side of his nature and sought the feminine or the soft, warm protection, like a place of new birth.

Without knowing it or terming it as such, Francis was looking to find inside these dark, secure dwellings a place to rest. Like a spiritual climber up high in the mist on a mountain that extends from the top of his head to the summit in the heavens, to the bottom of his feet and beyond to the scree in the tortures of hell, Francis sought to bivouac on ledges and cavelike places when the storms of doubt and uncertainty racked his human mortal nature. The storms of his soul were not unlike the storms that he knew so well on Mount Subasio where driving, lashing wind whipped his perches and threatened to toss him off the site like a ripped tent in hurricane-force wind. But still he held. When rain and hail pummeled him high on the veriglass ice of his unknowing, Francis did not slip. When thundering avalanches of personal ridicule pelted him as he walked the streets of Assisi beneath what used to be geranium-filled boxes of perfumed color and gaiety, he clung to the cold granite rock that warmed through its embracing. Francis' mountain became the desert places of so many spiritual ascetics who had gone before him. It was the parapet that the devil tempted Christ on and it was the endless sands that so many searchers had wandered upon–Abraham, David, John–seeking that one moment when the leap is made into solid footing, the bivouac that can be dug out of because the storm is over and the skies are cleared and the sun clearly shows the path before him. The moment the crucifix spoke, Francis' leap was fortified. His decisions were confirmed, his way clarified.

OUR RESPONSE

Who would not have loved to have been there for that moment, to breathe one lung full of that most rarefied air in the chapel of San Damiano when the crucifix spoke the *ruah* of God to Francis? It must have been a lung full of oxygen so rich it lasted him a lifetime. This air and this moment fueled an inner journey akin to transforming matter into spirit. Francis wanted to be among the angels in the heavens, so he could perpetually be near his Lord. What about us?

Do we really "get it"? Do we see that to be true followers of the dream we must make this inner walk to confront and convert our own demons? I know an alcoholic who after an accident literally stopped dead in his tracks and came to the sobering realization that he "got it" and didn't need to deaden (through drinking) all his feelings of loneliness and rejection. Granted, this realization came in the midst of the trauma of court hearings, license suspension, humiliation, fear of incarceration and literally being forced into his interior cave by all the outside forces of life. Nevertheless, he realized he had to pick himself up off the ground with his own arms and he had to walk himself over to Jesus' arms.

We, too, must come to this realization, or one like it. This is our calling here on earth as disciples—to convert the matter, the physical nature of ourselves, into spirit. Granted we cannot actually convert matter to spirit, but we *can* convert our thinking and the interior way we look at things to assimilate the spiritual into our daily life experience.

These interior journeys can be made every day. We don't need a cave to run to on our vacation—as Francis tells us, we carry our cell within. Each and every day, we need only place our *awareness* and our *intent* in this place, and we begin the path of revamping and transforming our daily existence. We then slowly become more spirit than flesh. We slowly become the instruments that Christ told us to become, with the influence over matter that he tells us is ours—if we embrace it and do it! Christ tells us to heal the sick, raise the dead and to do even greater things than he did. How? By entering in, by walking through the doorway and listening in the quiet niches of our souls. By placing our intent on acting more Christlike the transformation has already begun. We become part of this group of angels not because we are praying and begging them to intervene—we become part of this celestial group because we are changing it ourselves.

NOTE

[1] Murray Bodo, *Francis: The Journey and the Dream* (Cincinnati: St. Anthony Messenger Press, 1988), p. 8.

CHAPTER TEN

OF SHELLS, HEAVEN, SKY AND PILGRIMAGE

THE CROSS

The predominant colors of the San Damiano crucifix are black, red and gold. Black, which should come as no surprise, is symbolic of death. Red the color for life—as in blood—the body's lifeline. And gold is a regal color.

There is symbolism in the colors of the robes on the figures also; for example, the women are robed in red as symbols of life. And, there are cream-colored scallop shells all around the edge of the crucifix.

FRANCIS' RESPONSE

The cross of San Damiano is a cross of movement—alive, risen. It is not stilled by the nails embedded in flesh. The corpus is watching, and the characters on the cross have a life, a story to them. They and it are communicating, so that when you look at the cross, life is evident. The shells celebrate this life from the depths of the deep to the highest heavens; they appear on the cross as filigree, as extravagance. They are the countless musical notes of a celestial score; a symphony in waves and sand that roll and give themselves up for the ages.

One interesting aspect of the cross is that it is believed to have been painted by a Syrian monk. According to Franciscan Brother Joseph Wood, there were Eastern monks that were displaced or exiled in Umbria a hundred years before Francis.

These monks brought their art with them and influenced the region with their craftsmanship. Like the Greeks and Eastern peoples two thousand years before Francis, the monks sailed the Mediterranean in search of places for new settlements (in their case, for new monasteries) and brought their craftsmanship with them. Similarly, the ancient Etruscans, whose architecture, tombs and influences are rich in the Umbrian region as well as in the coastal areas above Rome, were prolific artisans intrigued with Greek art and vase painting. The idea that artisans and monks brought their culture and customs to this region of Italy is not unique or unusual. The cross and its combination Byzantine, Romanesque and Umbrian heritage would not have been out of place. In fact, these aspects of the cross add to its uniqueness and perhaps contributed to drawing Francis to its presence.

Our Response

Brother Joseph Wood talks of these shells, which embellish the edges of the cross, in terms of the boundless fruit of the seas that are symbolic of heaven. I have also read that the shells are symbolic of the sky—not heaven in particular—but the endless sky, again building on the plentiful theme of billions of shells on the beach. There is also an image from the Middle Ages of conch shells representing pilgrimage and frequently seen in frescoes being held by pilgrims to symbolize the far reaches of their journey and the trials they have gone through.

The multiple images of plentitude, travel, boundlessness, heavens and the sky need not be separate in meaning. The symbolism of the shells can be a collective imagery of the countless souls that have traveled beyond the terra to the skies and hopefully to heaven. The collective image of the shells seems to me to be the mystery of seashells in the first place. The mystery of what they are: the beauty, the presence, the uniqueness, the very reason why we stop and look, reach down and pick them up.

I have a tray of the most special shells on my kitchen table. Throughout my house are other bowls and displays of seashells that I have collected throughout the years. They are like jewels to me. I have been collecting them for decades, and they never cease to amuse and amaze me. They remind me of the wonder of creation and a God who would fancy such whimsy. I love the idea of a God who lavishes billions of seashells on a beach for me to walk over. I love the idea of a God who places them in the crags of coral reefs for me to study and pause over as I snorkel by. I love the idea of a God who brings these items forth from a sea through tides guided by the moon and sun, storms and calm. This God is a God of rhythm, a God of seasons, a God who is dynamic in nature and not static.

It is no wonder that shells surround the cross and decorate its edges, framing the story in, hemming up the sides. Our lives rest within such boundaries. We are of finite existence on this earth, our lives framed by the beauty of creation that surrounds us. We are among the figures painted with the shells of the San Damiano crucifix—we need only look into them, and we are there.

CHAPTER ELEVEN

ROCK AT THE FOOT OF THE CROSS

THE CROSS

The San Damiano crucifix sits on stone, presumably the rock of
Golgotha and the rock of Saint Peter from Christ's words, "And
I tell you, you are Peter, and on this rock I will build my
church…" (Matthew 16:18). The lower portion of the cross has
other figures which cannot be made out because the paint is
flaking off. Popular legend tells us this paint is missing due to
the devotion of those kissing Christ's feet or perhaps weeping at
this part of the cross because it is closest to the ground and
could be easily reached by any worshiper.

FRANCIS' RESPONSE

Francis gave up Pietro Bernardone as his father, yet sought the
shelter and protection of another Pietro—San Pietro, Saint Peter.
I have always wondered if in Francis' mind he was giving up one
Pietro, his earthly father, for the more spiritual father in Christ's
appointed representative, Saint Peter, and the vicars and successors of Saint Peter—the popes.

Francis sought the shelter of the church of Rome where he
went as a pilgrim and first exchanged clothes with a beggar. He
went to Rome to ask Pope Innocent III to approve his way of life
and his rule—and more. As poet and writer Murray Bodo unveils
in *Francis: The Journey and the Dream*:

Innocent in fact did more. He rose from his throne and embraced Francis, and Francis felt through the rich papal garments the beating of a poor and ragged heart like his own, who longed to change places with any one of these beggars and fools of Christ. Francis wept aloud, not only for the joy that the Dream was real, but because the touch of this man was the softness he had always longed for from his own father. The Pope had become more than the tangible representative of Christ. He was the father he had lost, given back a hundredfold.[1]

Pope Innocent III, one of the successors of Peter who was the rock of the church and the closest mortal to Christ on earth, had honored Francis before all the cardinals. Not even his earthly father Pietro Bernardone, who must have been intimidating since the name means "Big Bernard" or "Peter of the Big Bernard," could negate the blessing of the successor of Peter on his son. The pope's blessing was absolute. Francis and his followers were formally within the fold. And Francis, ironically, was to be another rock on which Innocent III dreamed the church of St. John Lateran, the mother church of Christianity, would be supported.

In essence, the stones Francis laid in place at San Damiano, the rock at the foot of the cross that is Calvary, the rock here at the base of the San Damiano crucifix, the rock of Peter and the church of Christ, are all of one lineage—a lineage of grace metamorphosing the essence of our world into symbols of the next world. Francis saw the symbols and understood them as signposts. He could touch the rocks and hear them sing because he did not elevate himself above the seemingly lowly. He embraced all things discarded. He was as much at home in an open field of wildflowers under Brother Sun as in a pigsty of mud and twigs, or in a cave. His was a life that did not limit itself to the normal mortal boundaries that we set upon our lives by our houses, cars, jobs and roads. He sought to transcend boundaries and walk with a foot in this world and a foot in the next. He sought to merge with Christ by being Christlike. This sounds simplistic, but imagine what it must have been like for a human to alter his ego strength and perception of self—which we all strive to advance and glue together in order to make what we perceive to be a successful traverse of our life. We all try to extend the inner vision of ourselves. Francis, in contrast, sought to hone his ego, his self, in order to be humble—to be *less*, not more. This is contrary to human nature and is of the realm of the mystical.

OUR RESPONSE

When I first knelt in front of the San Damiano crucifix in Assisi I remember seeing all the figures on the cross, the symbolic family gathered around Christ, and I wondered how was it that Francis could claim this cross as a symbol of his new life and listen to its commands when he had insulted his own father? I remember being puzzled by his finding solace in giving his father's treasures away—as if they were his. It came to me that Francis was shedding his inheritance, not his possessions. The riches he so lightly cast off were his father's, not his own. Casting off his inheritance was no small matter, mind you, but not so great an issue as if he had truly given up his *own* possessions that he had worked hard for—as his father had worked for and provided.

The impetuous young Francis never grew to old age to feel the chasm that the young—in avid pursuit of their own life—cast between generations. It is a lesson that we, as the "matured" lineage of Francis, can rectify in our own lives—that we work daily and steadfastly to bring the lepers of our lives to our family table, especially the lepers within our own family already sitting in our midst, whose placemats at the table are already set, whose lives we owe our own to. We must not exclude or marginalize—nor throw the treasure of them aside for some others—even in the name of God as Francis did. I am certain that this was only the rash action of youth and that the mature Francis—had he lived—would have embraced the "leper" that he had made of his father. And how quick, therefore, we should be to encourage reconciliation at every turn because time is not of our control. We think we have "all the time in the world" to do this or that, finish this or that, or take care of this or that—but we don't know when the final hours will be.

Christ tells us that no one knows when the final hours are, and perhaps we come to think that this is overly dramatic to think in terms of the end of the world—but actually, we see small unexpected "ends" all the time that we don't recognize as such until it is too late. For instance, what about when we attend a class reunion and make so many promises to see our friends here and there—with all good intentions to do so—and then never see them? We didn't know that when we were with them that that would be the last time we would ever see them. Time is precious and must be utilized, particularly in the essences of love, forgiveness, friendship, family ties. Love and relationships are tenuous and need care to remain gardens of solace, healing and relaxation. We too carelessly abandon these gardens or don't administer to them the care they deserve, and bitterness and anger grow like weeds within.

As Christ washed the feet of his disciples to symbolize humility, presence and love—so should we symbolically "kiss one another's feet" to the extent that, as with the San Damiano crucifix, we are literally wearing the paint off the surface. I think all of us and everyone we know would prefer to have a loving action given to us that "wears down some of our surface paint" in the name of care and devotion than not.

NOTE
[1] Bodo, p. 37.

CHAPTER TWELVE

OF HANDEDNESS

THE CROSS (RIGHT SIDE)

Under Christ's arms are angels. And at the right side of Jesus stands Mary, the Virgin Mother of God, and John. Both of their hands are pointing toward Jesus, and he is turned slightly toward them. In the Eastern church, being at God's right hand is the place of honor, the sign of blessedness. Mary and John are the chosen figures in the San Damiano crucifix, just as they were on Calvary when Jesus said to his mother, "Woman, here is your son" (John 19:26). And, when he looked at John and said, "Here is your mother" (John 19:27).

FRANCIS' RESPONSE

It would be logical to assume that Francis would place his name into Christ's directive to Mary and John the Beloved, "Woman, here is your son, [Francis]" and "[Francis], here is your mother." Francis would have wanted a spiritual family, particularly in the uncertainty of his first steps away from his own family into the realm of the church and all its trappings; Francis would have wanted to be on the right hand of God. He would have wanted to fit in, though it is a tall order to fit into the spiritual family of Christ and those present at the crucifixion.

Francis and his age of the thirteenth century had an extraordinary devotion to Mary, the mother of God. In the tiny town of Assisi there were in his lifetime two churches dedicated to Mary, Santa Maria Maggiore and St. Mary of the Angels on the plain below the city. Also, since history tells us that Francis was close to his mother (Lady Pica, who took food to him when his father imprisoned him in the family home), it would be easy for him to relate to the Mother of his Lord. He certainly would have identified with John the Beloved and would have wanted to be seen as Francis the Beloved, because of his own extreme love and identification with this moment of the passion. All the mortal questions were being answered right here at this moment of crucifixion, with Mary and John present in the earthly trilogy. Christ was leaving the earth, exiting his mortal form—and his mother, who gave birth to his mortal flesh, weeps at his feet, while his friend comforts her, and him. Family ties and bonds of friendship—two of the most powerful links of chain the universe can forge.

These relationships, mother and son and best friend and protector, would have intrigued Francis and beckoned to him, and perhaps at first, even haunted him. Who would be his spiritual mother? Who would be his devoted brother? Would anyone weep for him if this path he was embarking on led to ruin? He would have to chance it. He used to trust. Faith is a difficult mystery to embrace because it demands that we act in the future tense. Our actions are toward what we hope will be. This runs counter to human logic and experience yet is the essence of the spiritual. No doubt Francis snuggled himself among the figures there on the right hand of the cross hoping to be accepted, waiting for the first words of communication and recognition.

OUR RESPONSE

While I was sitting on the porch one day with my dying father, he unexpectedly asked me, "What do you suppose it means—to sit on the right hand of God? Who sits at the left hand of God?" The question has always haunted me, because I sensed he was concerned with where he personally would be sitting, and if one meant heaven and one meant hell. Therefore, the hands of the San Damiano cross being slightly elevated on the right has always seemed to me to indicate that even here, in this cross, there is a difference, a message. But what is it?

Though scholars might surmise a number of possibilities, the question of where we sit—that is to say where we are in relation to God—is beyond the study of sources and research. Our place, relative to God, can only be answered by us. Francis, when standing before the crucifix, would have had the same dilemma as my father had—where do I fit in? How do I know this? It is the deepest mortal question we can muster of ourselves when faced with the presence of the Almighty: Are we good, or are we bad? This is an interesting dilemma because we cannot really judge ourselves, yet we must. It haunts humankind through the ages, through what some might term the collective unconscious message from the Garden of Eden, namely, given the eternal love of God that surrounds us, why do we still sin? A wise friend once said to me that we are only as good as our worst sin. Interesting. For there are so many opportunities to pat ourselves on the back and see ourselves as good—when in fact we all fall so short of the mark—the mark that those like Francis set before us, the mark that the leper set before him.

Being great has nothing to do with success, fast cars or money; nor does it have anything to do with being big and tough or cool, or giving time and care to those in foreign lands, when, for example, we hurt the members of our immediate families. Francis' leper stood before him, right in front of him. Do we embrace the lepers that live right next door or right within the walls of our own home? Or do we self-righteously single out the lepers we want to be with while we make lepers of others and create pockets within our lives of only those who think like us and act like us?

My father's question about the right or the left hand of God was a good one. I have no doubt that Francis would have pondered the same issues. Humility makes us seek this self-introspection and analysis. Perhaps that is what Francis was doing at the end of his life when he lay at San Damiano and sang "The Canticle of the Creatures." Perhaps, even in his saintliness he knew it might well not be enough; for who is worthy? Certainly, no one.

The great fallacy of the religious person is to think that because one is religious, one is therefore better or made worthy. The message of Christ is that no one is worthy, no one at all. Yet how self-righteous we become when we declare that, "God said to me," or "God told me." I really wonder about statements like that—or about those who claim to have such a personal relationship with God that they know what God wants them to do and what is best for them and everyone else. One of the reasons I believe in Francis' credibility with his relationship or his encounter with the Holy is that he never tried to impose his beliefs on others. He simply lived the gospel and proclaimed its message; and at the hour of his death he said simply, "I have done what was mine to do—may the Lord show you what is yours."

Such humility is rare. That he, at San Damiano, while perhaps contemplating the cross within, called the elements his brothers and sisters, to identify his own place among the dirt of the earth and the nothingness of the stars, is amazing. It indicates to us that he saw himself as being miniscule, being created by someone infinitely greater than he, and above all, being imperfect. This lack of self-importance gave him a vision of self that left him wondering about his worthiness, left him wondering if he would sit on the left or the right hand of God.

This is the question we must all come to grips with at the time we truly become one with Christ. Are we as loving to the leper in our family whom we might have helped to create as we are with those we can visit and whose lives we can drop in and out of? Have we hurt our spouses? Have we hurt our mothers and fathers, sisters or brothers? Do we refuse to make amends because we are so proud that we know we are right and because we have been wronged or used, and therefore we have the right to be aloof, punishing and withholding of love to someone who wants it and desperately needs our forgiveness—but we won't give it?

The hands of the cross reach out with open palms to all— one higher, one lower. Only God can unravel that mystery of who sits where. But for us, it is our charge to order the palms of our hands to give the handshake that we have long withheld, to stroke the head of a sister or brother that we have struck in emotional or physical anger, to hold dear the life of our mothers or fathers, sisters and brothers as closely as we hold dear the lives of our children; to work with our hands as hard for the kingdom of God as we do for the kingdom of our own home and social status; to forgive and seek to make an opening for peace.

Take a good look at your hands and tell yourself what it is they do or don't do. This is the type of struggle Francis endured in contemplating the cross, I know this because it is the type of struggle all humans endure when faced with their own mortality. Our self-righteous nature fuels our decisions to reinforce our position. Yet the questions remain and symbolically were written onto the cross for us to ponder. Why are we here? Why was I created? Do I love enough and in the right way? Have I forgiven my brother or my sister? Have I embraced those that I made into lepers?

Will I sit on the right or the left?

THE CROSS (LEFT SIDE)
On the cross, at his left as on his right are three animated angels that seem to be chatting. Archangels? Raphael, Gabriel, Michael? We don't know, nor do we know what they are saying, yet they are intent on Christ's hands. The figures of Mary Magdalene, Mary Clopas and the Centurion, who declared Christ was the Son of God, stand at Christ's side. The Centurion has no halo, so is a pagan who is presumed saved by his witnessing and recognition of Christ. Above him is a small face—perhaps the artist; watching.

FRANCIS' RESPONSE
Did Christ's hands look like the hands of a carpenter? A laborer? Or were his hands frail-looking? We know that Francis was slight of build.

Would Francis have thought it artistically incorrect to see Christ's hands depicted as longer-fingered finery—soft—and too regal to work? Being a carpenter, Jesus would have cut his hands from time to time, perhaps nicked them, hit them with a mallet accidentally. Francis himself was entering into a life of much harder physical labor than the life he was leaving behind as the pampered son of a wealthy cloth merchant. The topography of Christ's hands would be heavily veined, muscular, and thick, his palms more rough than smooth. Michelangelo gives these qualities to the hand of God in the touch of Adam in the fresco of the Sistine Chapel, yet smooths them in the

cool subtleties of the marble of his famous Pieta. Each artist—
each imaginer, like Francis—fills in the blanks of his own vision.

OUR RESPONSE

These details are important to one who tries to fill in form with
imagination.

In the San Damiano crucifix the artist presents his imagination coupled with symbol. Christ's hands are open and raised,
symbolic of life and strength. I learned a blessing from a friend
of mine who is a devout Greek Orthodox and Third Order
Secular Franciscan. When he blesses himself he says, while
making tiny signs of the crosses with his thumb on his eyes, his
ears, his lips, his heart and his hands, "Bless my eyes, O Lord,
that I might see your glory, bless my ears that I might hear your
will, bless my lips that I may speak only your words, bless my
heart that I might love as you love, and bless my hands that I do
only your deeds."

Our hands try to bless as an extension of the grace we
receive, and we do so in a manner that we imagine to be holy.
We don't know in what fashion Jesus used his hands in blessing, in healing, in work, in resting on the gunnels of Peter's boat.
I think Jesus thoroughly enjoyed the physical nature of
strength, capability, power, creativity and usefulness. He probably marveled at the human experiences of his daily life.

If the figures are the archangels, what sense would they
have of mortal handedness? Would they marvel at the utility of
hands or find touch extraneous because their intuition would
preclude the physical moment of touching? It is an interesting
philosophical question, which many movies and writers have
explored, because wondering what the spiritual realm is like
pervades our consciousness. Francis most likely wanted or
longed to enter that spiritual essence, if for no other reason than

to escape the harsh existence of daily life in the thirteenth century. A world of darkness, no electricity to light up the forest or the caves, the faces of the lepers he chose to live with or the sea he crossed at night. Fire would dance on all of these but not if it was raining, or the ship was rolling so hard that flame pots were too dangerous for fear of catching the decks on fire. The spiritual world of white feathers, pure air, would have been as seductive to Francis as it is to us.

How many times do we wish to escape our twenty-first-century existence because it is harsh in paradoxical framework? In stark contrast to Francis' world we minimize the spiritual because we have conquered (or so we think) so many diseases, and we have created nuclear power to yield endless electricity. Why do we need the wings of angels to speed our desires along when we have private jets and space labs?

Perhaps we need to seek angels and the spiritual work even more because of our technology. This is not a new thought, but it is a profound realization when we grasp it, that we are called to be even more humble than Francis because we have expanded the physical boundaries and horizons of life on planet earth. As we become part of the heavens that Francis stared at and part of the ocean depths that he sailed across, we need to be even more spiritually astute and in tune with the forces of the universe because we have the ability quickly—in the speed of an atomic submarine—to alter existence, a concept Francis would not have even been able to conceive of.

How do we enter this awareness? What prayer do we have to recite? There is an ancient one that we can use to put into perspective and to bless whatever action we are undertaking:

Raphael cum Tobia,
Gabriel cum Maria,

Michael cum celeste curia,
protage te nos in via.

Loosely translated it means:

Raphael with Tobias,
Gabriel with Mary,
Michael with all the heavenly choirs of angels,
protect us along our way.

This prayer solicits the three archangels and all the heavenly hosts to be with us, and therefore for *us* to be among *them* during whatever action we are performing, whether it be driving, working, having dinner, attending a baseball game or piloting a jet. It is a great visual cue to keep us aware that we were not created, nor intended to be, one-dimensional.

CHAPTER THIRTEEN

CREATURES

THE CROSS

The cock or rooster can be seen on the left side near Christ's leg. Egyptians used the rooster for the harkening of the dawn; in Christian times it symbolized a call to lauds. The legends of Saint Francis include his meeting with the Wolf of Gubbio, his saving the lamb from being butchered, his sermon to the birds, his love of his sisters, the lark; and the peacock that crowed so loudly he couldn't sleep. Also, in Umbrian legend there is the lore of the cock being used to warn the villagers of approaching armies, for the cock would be startled by advancing troops. This tradition gave rise to the popular "kitchen chicken." In Italy, many Umbrian and Tuscan vases and potteries have a stylized chicken or cock painted on them with elaborate tail feathers. Adding to the richness of the folklore, the rooster stands for luck and good health, as when in a legend from 1561 Guiliano dei Medici was said to have been saved from assassination by the crowing of a rooster.

The artist of the cross no doubt had many reasons to include the rooster, not the least being that the rooster recalls the denial of Peter (see Matthew 26:69–75).

Francis' Response

Brother Thomas of Celano records the story of "The Cock and the Little Black Hen" in which Francis has a dream of a black hen with feathered feet who has so many chicks surrounding her that she cannot get all of them under her wings. Francis awakes and is led by the Holy Spirit to interpret the dream as his followers being the chicks and he the little black hen who cannot protect the flock and seeks the greater protection of Mother Church.

In his book, *Saint Francis: Nature Mystic*, Edward Armstrong has done a masterful job of researching the sources of Francis or Franciscan legend that speak of larks, cuckoos, turtledoves, doves, nightingales, swallows, wolves, waterfowl, dogs, cats, asses, bees, cicadas, worms, fish, reptiles and of course all the animals present in the manger, a tradition which Francis started at Greccio.[1]

But it is with birds that we most associate Saint Francis, whose image adorns countless birdbaths throughout the world. Here is his Blessing of the Birds:

> My brothers, birds, you should praise your Creator very much and always love him; he gave you feathers to clothe you, wings so that you can fly, and whatever else was necessary for you. God made you noble among his creatures, and he gave you home in the purity of the air; though you neither sow nor reap, he nevertheless protects and governs you without any solicitude on your part.[2]

Our Response

Throughout the ages birds have mesmerized us. Greek mythology tells us that Icarus tried to fly to the sun like a bird with wings of wax, but the wings melted when he got too close to the heat of the sun. Leonardo de Vinci drew wings in his sketchbook hundreds of years before the Wright Brothers flew at Kitty Hawk. Saint Francis of Assisi would have been inundated with Etruscan paintings of elaborate feathered birds like peacocks and roosters, and chickens would have been part of everyday existence.

But we, in our removed world of steel buildings, air-conditioning and windowless supermarkets, do not walk among the chickens in the morning to gather eggs. We don't rely on roosters to signal alarms of approaching armies or intruders. Ours is an electronic world of buzzers and red flashing lights, eggs that come in plastic or foam cartons. A rooster heralding the dawn? Not likely to be part of our daily lives unless we live on a working farm or in parts of the tropics where chickens walk freely. We live more isolated from nature than our parents or our grandparents, and at what cost?

The environmental costs of seeing and acting as if we are removed and somehow above, or worse, in control, of our environment can cause staggering consequences, as we have seen in recent years of hurricanes, global warming, tsunamis and global natural disasters. The sense of being removed and secure in our office buildings and multimillion-dollar homes is artificial. We live in stark contrast to Francis and those of the Middle Ages, or of those in the time of Christ. Without the feel of the warm underbelly of a hen against our flesh that we have just reached beneath to check for an even warmer egg, what reverence do we place on a live chicken? Do we get the same appreciation for the life of a chicken when we peel the plastic off the top of frozen chicken tenderloins and pop them in the microwave? I don't think so, yet we must not lose that tangible proximity to such basic ancient life and forms and creatures.

Birds in the air or eggs from a chicken are ancient groundings that center and focus our world. Bird flight overhead grounds us to the earth. We are bipedal. We do not fly unless artificially enhanced by propellers, jet motors or gliders. We are grounded to this earth, which we so frequently try to cover over with hardwood floors, linoleum, tile–anything but dirt. We do not gather eggs from hens; we purchase them in well-lit supermarkets. We do not listen for roosters to sound alarms or to tell us the dawn is arriving. Instead, we use buzzers (and then promptly press the snooze button). As we look at the San Damiano crucifix, at this cock, a tiny representation of creaturehood deemed so important by the artist as to place it permanently on this cross, perhaps we should ask the question–would we? What might we place at Christ's leg to symbolize our awakening? A friend's story? A life-changing event? One of our family pets that stayed with us when family members no longer visited? The rooster is a symbol, and it is important for us to select meaningful symbols in our lives that mirror those on this ancient cross to render for us a modern version–if only in our imagination–of the personalized moment that Francis was "awakened" by Christ and that we are invited to enter into also.

NOTES

[1] Edward Armstrong, *Saint Francis: Nature Mystic: The Derivation and Significance of the Nature Stories in the Franciscan Legend* (Berkeley, Calif.: University of California Press, 1973), pp. 81–84.

[2] *Omnibus*, "Celano, First Life," 58, p. 278.

CHAPTER FOURTEEN

CLEAR SAILING

THE CROSS

At the top of the crucifix, above Christ's head is a circle inside that Christ is clearly walking, for one foot is on the circle's rim and one is elevated in the air as if he is taking a step. This symbol of movement always fascinated me when I looked at the cross years ago in Assisi. The circle traditionally represents perfection, and Christ's presence in it symbolizes that he is perfect. There are three circles, with the top smallest one bisected by the top edge of the cross. The next one is of Christ walking and is larger, and the last, the halo of Christ, is the largest and brightest of the three as if to symbolize the all-cumulative nature of the resurrected Christ. But it also struck me that the circle—unusual on a cross—might also be the earth, the universe or a compass. We know that Christ, empowered with the Holy Spirit walked on the water to Peter in the boats at the Sea of Galilee. Where is Christ walking to here? Is he leading us across this ancient symbol of the beyond—the element to be crossed to conquer ourselves? To conquer death?

FRANCIS' RESPONSE

Surely Francis felt lost and wondered at times, as in the many times he returned to San Damiano, and to Assisi, after he had drifted aimlessly into uncharted waters, without the spiritual wind driving him forward, filling his soul with confidence, clarity and strength.

We know that Francis suffered many doubts and troubled times. When the wind leaves the sail, there is a hollow, eerie flap as the sail lofts in the breeze and the momentum slows to a halt. When the human spirit lofts in the wind, it is painful and draws one into introspection—as with Francis entering caves to pray. The San Damiano crucifix was his driving wind that filled his sails and gave him momentum. And he must have looked carefully in the various quadrants of his life for its signs.

What must it have been like for him to walk through the city gates of Assisi and go outside the protective walls? And what must it have been like to return and come back when he had seen Egypt and Rome and had to face the stares of a very small town where his uniqueness could not be hidden? The cross might have been a door for him, a portal into another world—a world he tried to tread in while still on earth. Perhaps one reason Francis took his itinerant-preacher-on-the-road stance for himself and his brothers, rather than the stationary Benedictine monastery way of life, was the walking Christ on the San Damiano crucifix. If Christ was going to be in motion and travel, then surely Francis would want to do the same.

His travels included physical trips as well as the uncertainty of being a pilgrim and a stranger in a strange land. He sought the hard way, the way of discomfort, poverty and danger because the more comfortable way, complete with the amenities of the age, was to not be a follower of his crucified Lord. Francis was a man who had seen the corruption of the church through ecclesiastical trappings and princely excesses, and he wanted none of it. He wanted to literally follow in the footsteps of Christ, and Christ's steps could be seen literally and figuratively on the top of the San Damiano crucifix.

Our Response

Following in the footsteps of Christ—literally taking the calling of being a Franciscan and walking off the painted surface of this scenario, embracing the crucifixion, and stepping into our current world—is a challenge. And for each person the challenge will be unique, just as it was for Francis. Each path will be different, some circuitous, some more direct. Some will take extraordinary journeys while others may never leave the rails of a hospital bed. Each journey is singularly important and critical to the mystery of being a living part of the body of Christ.

As for me, I have sailed over ten thousand miles. And I have learned to look for what I cannot see, such as wind. I learned to tell the effects of wind—a light rustle in the sail or coolness on my cheek. I learned to watch for the cat paws kneading the water surface along. Strong wind is easily deciphered, though sometimes perilous. The subtle, gentle wind is most often present and more comforting. I do think Francis sat and waited to read the wind—the spirit—walking softly toward him to fill his sail with grace and hope and presence—enough, just enough to carry his purpose along the journey, through the waters.

Navigation requires looking in quadrants, studying the slice of water or air carefully and then moving a few degrees around to the next quadrant. A good sailor does not scan the horizon aimlessly. A good sailor looks at one piece of the view, analyzes it, and then moves to the next piece of the view. Francis must have had some of these qualities to navigate the tricky waters of the church, his family, the bishop, even the demons within his own mind. He must have had some of these qualities to enter in and leave the gates of Assisi—or to pass through the doors into the chapel of San Damiano. He had to navigate carefully, certainly joyfully at times, but also in spiritual awareness that he was a disciple of Christ and because he had chosen this path, would surely suffer at times for it. For when a sail is full with wind, steerage is easy and a sense of strength envelops the boat. But when the wind slips away, and you didn't know it was leaving, the loss can leave you bereft. And like Francis, when we lose our way we must return to the place of our making—the foot of the cross—and beg for guidance, steerage and wind.

CHAPTER FIFTEEN

THE CANTICLE OF BROTHER SUN

THE CROSS

Christ is the image of the invisible God that Francis fell in love with and embraced. Saint Paul's Letter to the Colossians explains this invisible God to us:

> He is the image of the invisible God, the firstborn of all creation; for in him all things in heaven and on earth were created, things visible and invisible, whether thrones or dominions or rulers or powers—all things have been created through him and for him. (Colossians 1:15–16)

FRANCIS' RESPONSE

Francis fell in love with the invisible God. This is the being that Francis experienced in faith and in reality. What is the invisible nature of God? Does it mean that God is in absence because there is nothing there, like a negative connotation? Or does the invisible nature of God depict an elasticity of perception? We perceive God to be of a certain nature, but the nature of God is known only by God, and we are told in the Letter to the Colossians, as Francis was told, that part of the nature of God is invisibility. God's invisible nature would mean that God is able to be where we cannot see him or don't experience or expect him. The invisible nature of God could mean that the face of our enemy is really the image of Christ. The cloak of perception drapes over the world's eyes, and who would see?

Why did Francis see and his father did not? What part of the fabric of God did Francis hold in his fingers or kiss with his lips that removed the invisibility, so as to press flesh to spirit? Francis entered into a realm of love when he entered into the world of the spirit of God and could see as he had not before, understand as he had not before, that the invisibility of God means that we can cloak ourselves in its malleable nature and walk without fear.

An invisible God crosses all boundaries because no one can claim it as his or hers alone. And so Francis' inclusiveness began in the comprehension that the invisible God encompassed all of creation.

Perhaps Francis' embrace and understanding of the concept of creaturehood, of being created, came from his encounter with the San Damiano crucifix. Its images are of humans, creatures, seashells, heavens and angels—indeed all orders of thrones—symbolically painted on this cross. The story of Francis' composition of "The Canticle of the Sun" reflects his insight into the universality of invisibleness, and is best retold in the Franciscan sources:

> Two years before his death, already very sick and suffering especially from his eyes, he was living in a cell made of mats near San Damiano. The minister general, seeing that his case was serious, ordered him to accept help and care. Moreover, he told him that he wanted to be present when the doctor began the treatment in order to see to it that he received the proper care and to comfort him, for he was suffering greatly.

But at that time it was very cold and the weather was not propitious to begin the treatment.

The Canticle of the Sun

During his stay in this friary, for fifty days and more, blessed Francis could not bear the light of the sun during the day or the light of the fire at night. He constantly remained in darkness inside the house in his cell. His eyes caused him so much pain that he could neither lie down nor sleep, so to speak, which was very bad for his eyes and for his health. A few times he was on the point of resting and sleeping, but in the house and in the cell made of mats, that had been made ready for him, there were so many mice running around here and there, around him and even on him, that they prevented him from taking a rest; they even hindered him greatly in his prayer. They annoyed him not only at night but also during the day. When he ate, they climbed up on the table, so much so that he and his companions were of the opinion that it was a diabolical intervention, which it was.

One night, as he was thinking of all the tribulations he was enduring, he felt sorry for himself and said interiorly: "Lord, help me in my infirmities so that I may have the strength to bear them patiently!" And suddenly he heard a voice in spirit, "Tell me Brother, if, in compensation for your sufferings and tribulations you were given an immense and precious treasure: the whole mass of the earth changed into pure gold, pebbles into precious stones, and the water of the rivers into perfume, would you not regard the pebbles and the waters as nothing compared to such a treasure? Would you not rejoice?" Blessed Francis answered, "Lord, it would be a very great, very precious, and an inestimable treasure beyond all that one can love and desire!" "Well, Brother," the voice said, "be glad and joyful in the midst of your infirmities and tribulations: as of now, live in peace as if you were already sharing my kingdom."

"...God has given me such a grace and blessing that he has condescended in his mercy to assure me, his poor and unworthy servant, still living on this earth that I would share his kingdom. Therefore, for his glory, for my consolation, and the edification of my neighbor, I wish to compose a new "Praises of the Lord," for his creatures. These creatures minister to our needs every day; without them we could not live; and through them the human race greatly offends the Creator. Every day we fail to appreciate so great a blessing by not praising as we should the Creator and dispenser of all these gifts." He sat down, concentrated a minute, then cried out: "Most high, all-powerful, and good Lord...." And he composed a melody to these words which he taught his companions.... [1]

(See Appendix B for "The Canticle of Brother Sun.")

OUR RESPONSE

And so, the Lord spoke to Francis twice at San Damiano, once at the beginning of his life in the Lord and now near the end. Did he come here for consolation because he had found it once before? What relationship do we embrace with the invisible God? With our creaturehood? One must be humble to accept having been created, because it demands that there is something greater than we. I know that is why I walk by the sea. The invisibleness of God touches me most there, in that ethereal medium. The sea, like God, seems eternal, the waves endless in repetition, the sand and the surface changing yet always the same.

Do we walk on the sand and look out to sea in thanksgiving? Or do we more likely walk on the sand in search of answers? For me the sea—whether angry or calm—has an allure that beckons me to stop, plant my feet into the rushing waves and down into the sand as the water carves a hollow for my feet—as if to capture me—even for a second—stilled to search out there on the horizon somewhere for something that I've never seen, yet something I know exists, that I will recognize instantly. It lies out there somewhere waiting for us. Francis knew this and he was in constant harmony with the moment of revelation, the proximity of the invisible Other.

NOTE
[1] *Omnibus*, "Legend of Perugia," 42–43, pp. 1020–1021.

CONCLUSION

In September 1224, Francis joined the crucifix, which spoke to him at San Damiano. While at La Verna, a mountain retreat in Tuscany, around the time of the feast of the Holy Cross, near dawn, Francis was praying,

> My Lord Jesus Christ, I pray You to grant me two graces before I die: the first is that during my life I may feel in my soul and in my body, as much as possible, that pain which You, dear Jesus, sustained in the hour of Your most bitter Passion. The second is that I may feel in my heart, as much as possible, that excessive love with which You, O Son of God, were inflamed in willingly enduring such suffering for us sinners.[1]

At that moment there, in the desolate woods, he saw a six-winged seraph—an angelic flame of love—come toward him; and when his eyes opened, he saw he had received the stigmata in his hands, in his side and in his feet.

This is perhaps the most significant impact of the cross on Francis: the human condition shared proximity with God. Like the larks in Assisi he soared beyond the empirical to the mystical—the realm of the divine, and he invites us to join him. This invitation is but one side of a two-sided coin: on the one side, human, and on the other side, the Other or the divine. Through grace, we can experience the "stuff of energy." That "stuff" is the nature of the energy that moves us to go beyond our humanity and is made tangible when we find ourselves in proximity to God.

The moment of that closeness is the stuff of movement not unlike that which Aristotle describes in his description of God as the Prime Mover and the object of all desire. For us, as humans, to be within the proximity of such energy is to be within a force. We call it grace. Grace that transforms the physical experience into the spiritual and divine. These moments of proximity that encompass the energy that sets in motion events that are life-changing and life-altering singularly and globally are the touch of the Other.

What we do with that touch defines our destiny. To be "tapped" into what can only be described as the loftiest of all such societies has, as its own irony, the essential element of humility. For as creatures, as those which come from the Other, we are at best only one level from nothingness. And it is from this stance, which is not a stance at all, but rather a prostration, that we encounter the wonder of God's being—the God of pure energy, and the purple light of royalty that is never destroyed nor created by another.

This energy lives around us, within us and through us when we are moved by it toward God and toward goodness. This movement comes not from judgment or pride, but rather it comes about out of reverence, awe and penitence. The state of proximity is the edge of the coin of which the flip side contains the boundless universe of Love. This coin of beauty is an amalgamation of spirit on one side and flesh on the other, made one in the moment when God passes close by. The motion of God—the energy of kinesis when near—claims us and all our complexity as its heirs.

God is within us and we are in God, and therefore we are in one another. This connection is not conscious. We have our own egos and our own self-knowledge, history and story. Rather, this connection is a unification of the human element in us all, spread forth from the past to the present and to the future, the living essence of God and the mystical within.

Our proximity then, to the Creator, is ever present within. It reinforces that we are all brothers and sisters and neighbors through him and in him. Throughout history, these great moments of holiness are heralded by saints who move us along the path that much farther toward perfection and unity, the completed circle of resubmersion into the Holy. Saints are our lighthouses. Thrust up against the sky, they fetch the fabric of our collective nature, and move us forward to a new place, and this advances humankind. Great saints like Francis of Assisi are the visible images of this communion with the Holy. He became global because his nature was of a global source.

In Francis the proximity of the creative energy of God was tangible. This is evident in the stories of the manger at Greccio and in the lepers. It was as if the collective spirit of good and God said, "Enough!" Is there no one who will comfort my people? And the collective memory of the original union with God in the garden broke though the hardheaded nature of the medieval world, and Francis was its product. He could be nothing but a saint. His own nature would have been tortured (as we know it was) with, "Why me?" He saw himself as the greatest sinner, the smallest of the small, the poorest of the poor. He would be but one infinitesimal part of all those gone before all those present and future in God, because he was in the proximity of the Holy. And it is the nature of God, of the Holy, to be inclusive and seek oneness, to perfect and heal itself to progress toward unity and completion.

Why would God seek the infinitesimal? He didn't seek it. He is it. The collective finite particles of each of us are the Body of Christ; are the whole. We are the very fabric of God; we are the fabric that is God. The energy we experience as the uniqueness of self is really the multifaceted face of God. We are the momentary mortal aspect of God in our lifetime, and at the moment of our death, his spirit returns to its purest state, the energy of the Divine. This energy with our unique expression is the creativity of the Creator, and it flows through our mortal condition and waits at the portal of our freewill to flow harmoniously with all existence—past, present and future.

Our personality is a product of our human nature, infused with the divine, like Christ. We make choices. We cry. We love. We play. We laugh. We are God's face as athletes, actresses, plumbers, saints because we are extensions of the limitless possibilities of God expressing godliness to one another. Like the figures on the San Damiano Cross we are called to participate in the mystical.

NOTE

[1]*Omnibus,* "The Little Flowers of St. Francis: The Third Consideration: About the Apparition of the Seraph and the Imprinting of the Holy Stigmata on St. Francis," p. 1448.

ANOTHER VISION, ANOTHER VERSION

There is a Native American version of the San Damiano cross, with a male, Navajo Christ. It was painted in 1995 by Linda Benton, for the church at Tohatchi, New Mexico. A picture of the cross was sent to John Paul II who asked if it could be added to the Vatican collection, where it remains today. (And because Pope John Paul II had an interest in this cross, I have included other references of his to the San Damiano crucifix in this section.) It interests me because it symbolizes the unconscious, universal symbolism of this cross. The Navajo version depicts Christ as a Native American, with Mary the Mother of God, Mary Magdalene, Mary the mother of John, and John as Navajos. A United States Cavalry officer replaces the Roman centurion, the angels gathered above and looking downward are Native Americans, and a Franciscan friar and Spanish conquistador, in the corners, act as witnesses.

The tradition of the San Damiano crucifix has also entered Navajo sandpainting. It is interesting that two ancient human forms of expression—the cross and sandpainting—have crossed paths and flirted with one another, and formed an interwoven fabric within human consciousness.

Sandpainting, traditionally a Native American art used by elders and medicine men to aid the inner journey of self-discovery through the forests of pain, sickness and depression, uses colored sand to draw patterns and symbols that create an external expression of someone's inner world. The San Damiano crucifix, coming forth from the unconscious in sandpainting therapies, indicates that it has entered into and is part of the psychic fabric of human existence. For some, moreover, that a modern painter would superimpose a Native American iconographic story onto the cross reinforces the idea that this cross reaches across the centuries and the miles and the fences of civilizations as a unifier. The San Damiano cross speaks to many.

For more information please contact:
St. Mary Mission
P.O. Box 39
Tohatchi, NM 87325

APPENDIXES

APPENDIX A

Prayer Before the San Damiano Crucifix
by Murray Bodo, O.F.M.
(Note: Choir One and Choir Two can be adapted to men and women, old and young, left and right sides of the congregation.)

All:
Jesus, Our Lord and Brother,
as we begin again to rebuild your house,
enlighten the darkness of our hearts,
give us true faith, certain hope,
and perfect charity.
Give us sensitivity and knowledge,
Lord, that we might live your
holy and true command.

Choir One:
Mary, our sister and mother,
as you stand beneath the cross of your son,
help us rebuild the house of dignity and
equality in your Church, so that we might
carry your son through love and, like you,
give birth to him by holy acts that shine
as an example and model to others.

All:
All you holy angels, protect and sustain us
as we rebuild God's house

Choir Two:
John, our brother in what it means to love,

as you stand beside Mary, the mother of Jesus,
help us rebuild the house of relationships
between men and women in the world by
remembering that Our Lord, Jesus Christ,
included men and women in his ministry,
men and women like you who are faithful
and stand beneath his cross when others
flee from fidelity to relationship.

All:
All you holy women and men, intercede for us
as we build God's house.

Choir One:
Mary Magdalene, true lover of Jesus,
help us rebuild the house of our relationships
through love that forgives as we are forgiven,
through a deep, virginal love of Him
whose feet you washed with your hair.
Help us forgive those who would exclude
women from touching, equally with men,
the same Jesus in his Body, the Church.
Help us to be there when those same excluders
have fled the cross he hangs upon.

All:
All you holy Angels, protect and sustain us
as we rebuild God's house.

Choir Two:
Our brother, the anonymous Roman Centurion,
whose son was healed by Jesus, help us rebuild
the house of faith, even in the midst of war

that destroys the very sons and daughters whom
Jesus healed. Help us to not be afraid, but like you,
to keep faith, speak up against death and destruction,
and believe that Jesus can still heal sons and daughters
of war's destruction.

All:
All you holy men and women, intercede for us
as we rebuild God's house.

Choir One:
Mary, mother of James, help us rebuild the house
of humility falling into ruin through pride that makes
some want places of honor at the right and left hand
of Jesus. Help us stand, like you, in that place
beneath the cross abandoned by your son James
when leadership called him to walk the way of the cross
and watch his God die at the hands of the violent
and power-obsessed.

All:
All you holy angels, protect and sustain us
as we rebuild God's house.

Choir Two:
Our brother, the Centurion's son, standing behind
your father, help us rebuild the house of compassion
that sees and responds to those like you who suffer
and die because of our lack of faith. Help us to see
and believe, as your father did, that faith still heals,
that faith does not give up, that faith is obedient
to the healing power of Jesus.

All:
All you holy men and women, intercede for us
as we rebuild God's house.

Choir One:
Little rooster, almost hidden near the knee of Jesus,
help us rebuild the house of betrayal, by recalling
how you crowed when Peter had betrayed Jesus
three times. Help us to have courage and crow
when Jesus is betrayed outside and inside his church.
Help us rebuild the house of joy, as well, a new dawn
in the church, where men and women together crow
aloud the resurrection of Jesus from the bondage of
old restrictions and heavy burdens placed on God's
people.

All:
All you holy angels, protect and sustain us
as we rebuild God's house.

Choir Two:
Longinus, brave centurion who pierced the side
of Christ with a lance and proclaimed aloud,
"Truly this was the son of God," help us rebuild
the house of courage to proclaim God's presence
even when God seems dead, when violence destroys
what has been built up by holy men and women,
when God's Body is pierced by rape and pillage,
murder and genocide and war. Help us to be brave
and say aloud, "Truly this is God's own Body
that you have violated."

All:
All you holy women and men, intercede for us,
as we rebuild God's house.

Choir One:
Anonymous man, member of the Sanhedrin,
help us rebuild the house of reconciliation
by standing with those who do not believe
what we believe, with those whom we see
as the enemies of our own faith, whom we
believe are trying to destroy religion as we
understand it to be. Help us to be reconcilers
by being there, even in the "enemy's" camp,
even when we can only watch as the God
we love hangs seemingly helpless on the cross
of our inability to be reconciled with one another.

All:
All you holy angels, protect and sustain us
as we rebuild God's church.

Choir Two:
All you anonymous faces that are erased
beneath the feet of Jesus, help us rebuild
the house of remembrance. Let us not forget
those who have gone before us, those whose
names we've ceased calling upon, whose faces
are blurred by our reliance on the wisdom of our
own times and our preoccupation with the present.
Help us to be grateful for what we've been given.

All:
All you holy women and men, intercede for us
as we rebuild God's house.

Choir One:
Jesus, our brother, as you ascend to God,
your father and mother, help us rebuild
the house of contemplation by gazing
upon this crucifix preserved by our sister,
Clare. Help us once again to see and
respond to love overflowing.

All:
All you holy angels, protect and sustain us
as we rebuild God's house.

Choir Two:
Lord Jesus, our Beloved, help us rebuild
the house of our love. May the power
of your love, Lord Jesus, fiery and sweet
as honey, wean our hearts from all that
is under heaven, so that we may die for
love of your love, who died for love of
our love.

Choir One:
Amen. So be it.

Choir Two:
Amen. So be it.

All:
Loving God, our mother and father, hallowed be thy name, thy
kingdom come.

Appendix B

The Canticle of Brother Sun

Most High, all-powerful, all good, Lord!
    All praise is yours, all glory, all honour
    And all blessing.
To you, alone, Most High, do they belong.
    No mortal lips are worthy
    To pronounce your name.
All praise be yours, my Lord, through all that you have made,
    And first my lord Brother Sun,
    Who brings the day; and light you give to us through him.
    How beautiful is he, how radiant in all his splendour!
    Of you, Most High, he bears the likeness.
All praise be yours, my Lord, through Sister Moon and Stars;
    In the heavens you have made them, bright
    And precious and fair.
All praise be yours, my Lord, through Brothers Wind and Air,
    And fair and stormy, all the weather's moods,
    By which you cherish all that you have made.
All praise be yours, my Lord, through Sister Water,
    So useful, humble, precious and pure.
All praise be yours, my Lord, through Brother Fire,
    Through whom you brighten up the night.
    How beautiful is he, how gay! Full of power and strength.
All praise be yours, my Lord, through our Sister Earth, our
        mother,
    Who feeds us in her sovereignty and produces
    Various fruits with coloured flowers and herbs.
All praise be yours, my Lord, through those who grant pardon

For love of you; through those who endure
Sickness and trial.
Happy are those who endure in peace,
By you, Most High, they will be crowned.
All praise be yours, my Lord, through Sister Death,
From whose embrace no mortal can escape.
Woe to those who die in mortal sin!
Happy those She finds doing your will!
The second death can do them no harm.
Praise and bless my Lord, and give him thanks
And serve him with great humility.[1]

NOTE
[1] *Omnibus*, "Canticle of Brother Sun," p. 130.

BIBLIOGRAPHY

Armstrong, Edward. *Saint Francis: Nature Mystic*. Berkeley, Calif.: University of California Press, 1973.

Barret, C., F. Bodeur, C. Mahu and A. Perrin. *The Crucifix of San Damiano: A Way of Conversion*. Assisi: Fonteviva Editrice.

Bodo, Murray. *Francis: The Journey and the Dream*. Cincinnati: St. Anthony Messenger Press, 1988.

De Robeck, Nesta. *St. Francis*. Assisi: Casa Editrice Francescana, 1950.

Desbonnets, P. Theophile. *Assisi in the Footsteps of St. Francis: A Spiritual Guidebook*. Assisi: Libreria Fonteviva, 1982.

Englebert, Omer. *Saint Francis of Assisi: A Biography*. Cincinnati: Servant, 1979.

Fortini, Arnaldo. *Francis of Assisi: A Translation of Nova Vita di San Francesco*. Helen Moak, trans. New York: Crossroad, 1981.

Habig, Marion, ed. *St. Francis of Assisi: Writings and Early Biographies English Omnibus of the Sources for the Life of St. Francis*. Chicago: Franciscan Herald Press, 1973.

Picard, Marc. *The Icon of the Christ of San Damiano*. Assisi: Casa Editrice Francescana, 2000.

Sabatier, Paul. *Road to Assisi, The Essential Biography of St. Francis*. Edited by Jon M. Sweeney. Brewster, Mass.: Paraclete Press, 2003.

Saint Sing, Susan. *A Pilgrim in Assisi: Searching for Francis Today*. Cincinnati: St. Anthony Messenger Press, 1981.

Wilson, Michael. *Heads Bowed, Eyes Closed, No One Looking Around*. Covington, Ky.: What Reindeer Press, 1984.